The
Hindu
Temple

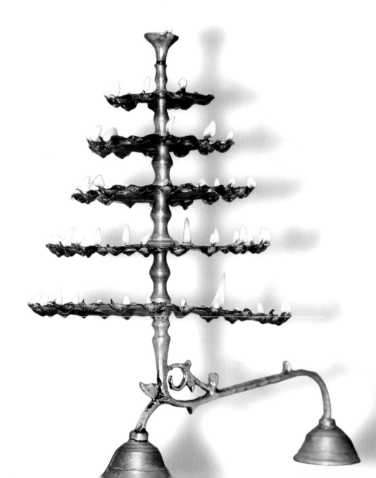

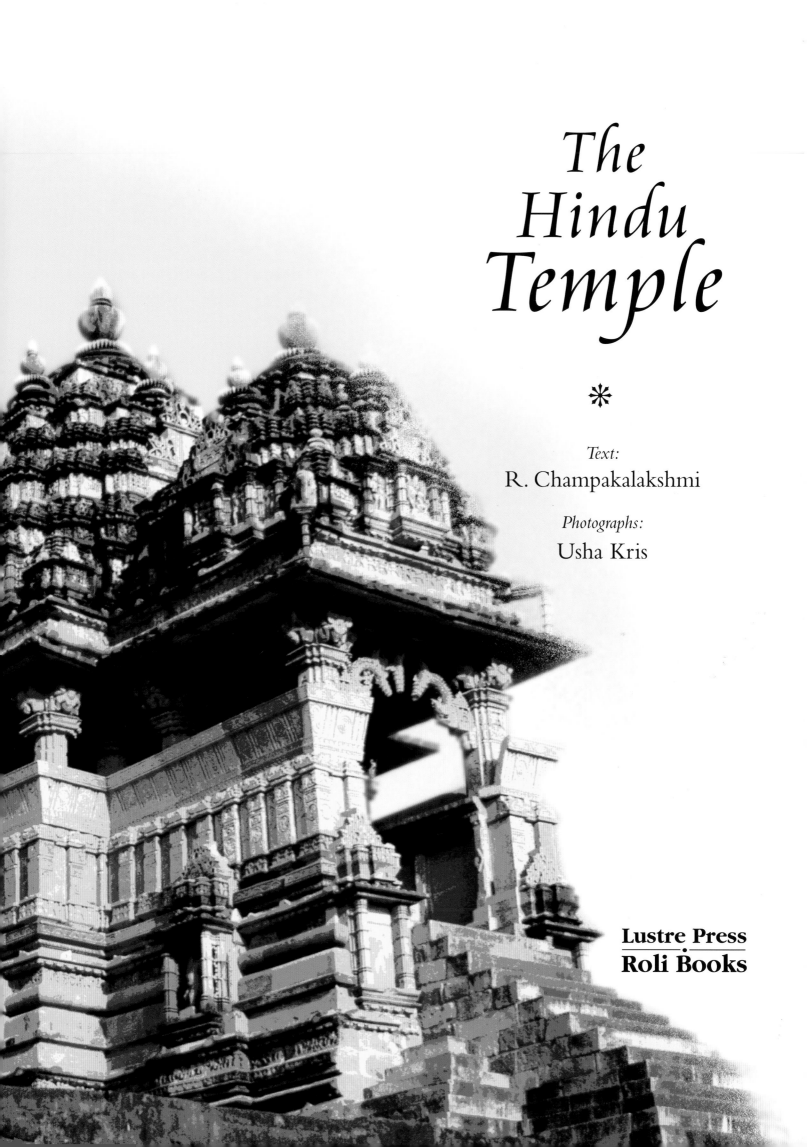

The Hindu Temple

*

Text:

R. Champakalakshmi

Photographs:

Usha Kris

Lustre Press
Roli Books

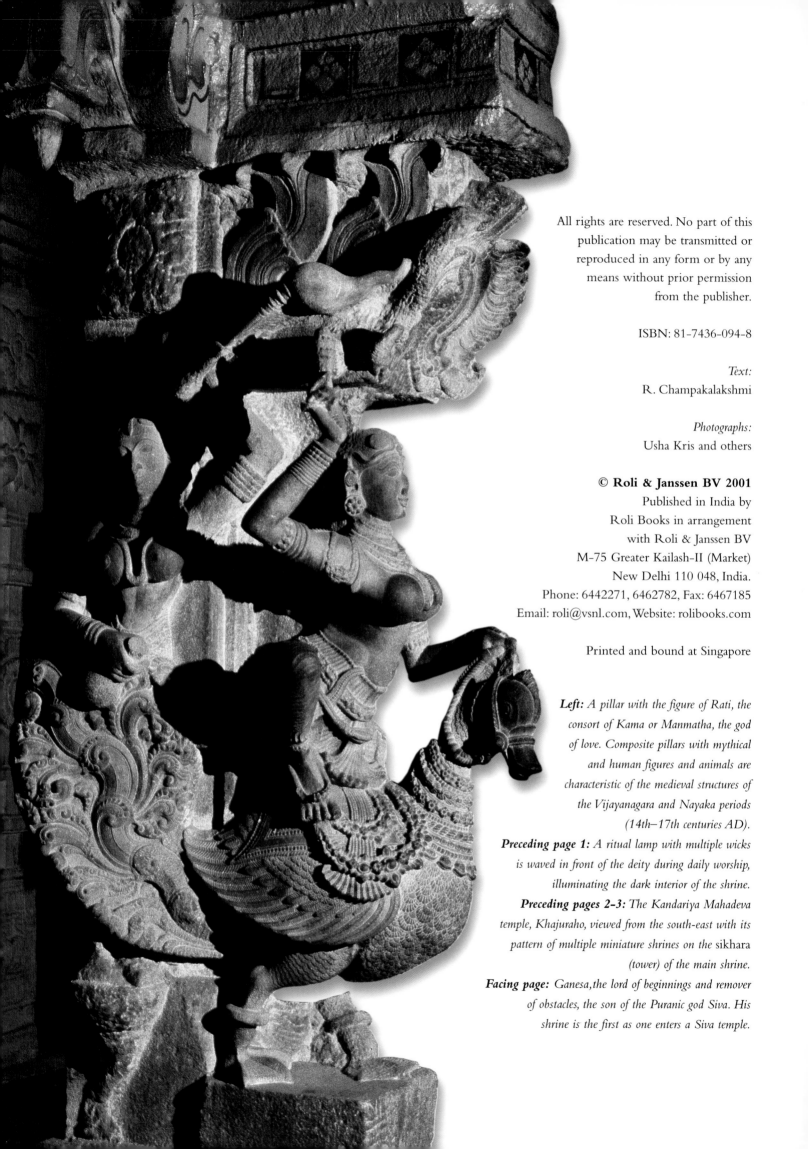

ISBN: 81-7436-094-8

Text:
R. Champakalakshmi

Photographs:
Usha Kris and others

© **Roli & Janssen BV 2001**
Published in India by
Roli Books in arrangement
with Roli & Janssen BV
M-75 Greater Kailash-II (Market)
New Delhi 110 048, India.
Phone: 6442271, 6462782, Fax: 6467185
Email: roli@vsnl.com, Website: rolibooks.com

Printed and bound at Singapore

Left: *A pillar with the figure of Rati, the
consort of Kama or Manmatha, the god
of love. Composite pillars with mythical
and human figures and animals are
characteristic of the medieval structures of
the Vijayanagara and Nayaka periods
(14th–17th centuries AD).*
Preceding page 1: *A ritual lamp with multiple wicks
is waved in front of the deity during daily worship,
illuminating the dark interior of the shrine.*
Preceding pages 2-3: *The Kandariya Mahadeva
temple, Khajuraho, viewed from the south-east with its
pattern of multiple miniature shrines on the* sikhara
(tower) of the main shrine.
Facing page: *Ganesa, the lord of beginnings and remover
of obstacles, the son of the Puranic god Siva. His
shrine is the first as one enters a Siva temple.*

Contents

Chapter 1

The Temple: A Symbol of Indian Culture

THE VISION OF A TEMPLE IN INDIA EVOKES AMONG HINDUS feelings of reverence, sanctity and spirituality as it symbolises an abode of God and a place of worship. Its origin goes back to the pre-Christian era, and its evolution into a monument of great architectural merit is marked by conscious efforts on the part of several ruling dynasties from the 4th to 17th centuries to make it an institution of enduring importance in the social, economic and political integration of the subcontinent. There are many regional variations in the process of its development as a symbol of Indian culture. Its historical past, therefore, makes a fascinating study both of its aesthetic significance and its role as the institutional focus of society and polity. Religion in India, needless to emphasise, has been a powerful ideological force, and hence the temple as the sacred and organised space for worship of the divine, served as the superordinate institution of societal organisation.

As a centre of worship, the temple is mainly a product and instrument of the Puranic tradition. Hindu myths, legends and beliefs are compiled in texts collectively called the Puranas; the Hindu pantheon of gods originated from the texts of two Brahmanical sects, the Vaishnava (those who worship Vishnu as supreme) and the Saiva (followers of Siva), which with other minor religious systems, are part of the Puranic tradition under what is now known as Hinduism. The Puranic tradition evolved out of a synthesis of the Sanskritic (Great/ Mainstream) tradition and the regional or vernacular (Little) traditions. This process of synthesis and assimilation is what is called Sanskritisation or the process of acculturation through the interaction between the Brahmanical forms of worship and the local, regional or vernacular forms of beliefs and practices or folk traditions. Despite the continuous process of acculturation and synthesis of these two traditions, folk / tribal forms persist in many ways – first, as part of the mainstream religious systems in their pantheons and rituals, and more importantly, as cult practices in private and public ceremonial worship and festivals, independent of the Brahmanical temple, with their own non-Brahmana priests and non-Brahmanical rituals. In almost every settlement, rural or urban, forest or hilly zones, this duality is conspicuously present in the places of worship – in major temples of the Puranic deities and in smaller cult centres of the local deities. For example, the cult of Vitthoba in Maharashtra, a survival of an early pastoral deity absorbed as a form of Krishna in mainstream Hinduism, still retains its tribal/folk origins and traditions. The cult of Khandoba, also in Maharashtra, similarly brings together all the pastoral tribes in the semi-forest and hilly areas for seasonal worship, although Khandoba has been identified as a form of Siva in the Hindu tradition. The cult of the mother goddess as Kali in Bengal, Bhagavati in

Preceding pages 6-7: A composite pillared hall (mandapa) with a shrine at one end and with ceiling decorations of the Nayaka period. Sculpture and paintings in mandapas increase in the late medieval temples. The pillars have mythical, human and animal figures.
Facing page: *Kapalisvara temple, Mylapore, Chennai. The idol of Siva with attending priests. The god is taken out in procession in full regal splendour on festive occasions.*

9

Khandoba, the pastoral-tribal deity of the Little Tradition or Folk Tradition in Maharashtra. He came to be identified with the Puranic deity Siva of the Great Tradition or Mainstream Religion of the Hindus.

Facing page: *Karuppannasami, a folk deity from Alanganallur near Madurai. His earthy folk character is reflected in his physique and ferocity. Propitiating him wards off evil and bestows success on the worshipper. The worship is conducted by local non-Brahman priests in keeping with the Little Tradition.*

Kerala and Mariyamman in Tamil Nadu retain their folk elements and cult centres despite the almost total merging of their identities in various localities with Durga or Parvati as the local consorts of Siva. Many more such phenomena are scattered in the rural areas of the Indian subcontinent.

Hinduism is a more recent nomenclature given to a conglomeration of heterogenous traditions and plurality of beliefs and worship with a long history of development from the Vedic (that which has originated directly from the Vedas – the four ancient texts which contain the core of Hindu philosophy and belief) sacrificial religion through the worship of epic and Puranic heroes and personal deities, cults and sects, as well as philosophical systems rather than to a monolithic tradition or a structure based on a single system of beliefs and worship or a single text as scripture. The temple, in more than one sense, represents the multiple facets and complex processes of this development through its architecture, sculpture, iconography, rituals and institutional organisation – it is like a text which has to be read and understood in the various contexts of its evolution into a monument of enduring value.

In the pre-modern periods of Indian history, the role of the temple as the institutional focus of development is underscored by the temple's social and economic outreach as a landowner, organiser of rural and urban activities, provider of educational and other facilities such as medical help and hospital, and above all, as the centre of cultural activities, such as the arts; painting and sculpture, apart from architecture; music and dance and more significantly as a symbol of political power. In the post-industrial period of worldwide economic growth and emergence of new world systems, the temple's role in economic activities has come to be conspicuously reduced, the capitalist instruments of change taking over the major aspects of economic development, and simultaneously, nationalist and democratic ideologies replacing almost totally the dominance of religious ideology in the political and economic spheres. The temple has been left with its ostensible function as a place of worship, while all secular aspects came to be separated, theoretically at least, from the religious. Yet, centuries of continuous domination enjoyed by the temple in society has helped to keep its traditional character alive and ensured its survival as a symbol of religious sustenance. Simultaneously, it has also become a viable instrument in the hands of communalist and fundamental forces which have tried to turn it into a symbol of Hindu nationalism.

It is the fascinating story of the temple's role as an integrative institution, and its contribution to the development of the creative arts such as architecture, sculpture, painting, music, dance, drama, and the allied arts, such as the crafts of bronze-casting, jewellery-making, and so on, that are highlighted in a work of this kind. Rituals, festivals and the idea of pilgrimages, that created a network of temple-centres and a sacred geography, continue to emphasise the integrative role of the temple in the subcontinent.

VASTUPURUSHAMANDALA

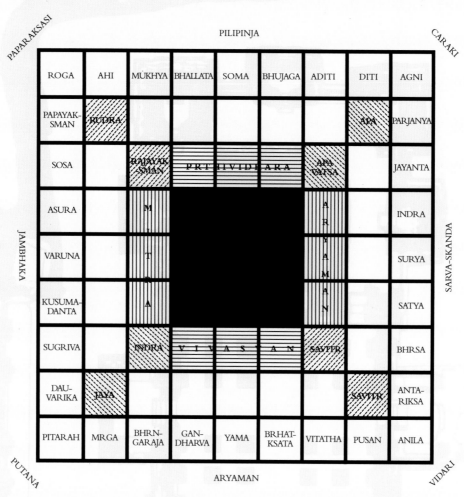

ROGA	AHI	MUKHYA	BHALLATA	SOMA	BHUJAGA	ADITI	DITI	AGNI
PAPAYAK-SMAN	RUDRA						APA	PARJANYA
SOSA		RAJAYAK-SMAN	PRTHIVIDHARA			APA VATSA		JAYANTA
ASURA		MITRA				ARYAMAN		INDRA
VARUNA								SURYA
KUSUMA-DANTA								SATYA
SUGRIVA		INDRA	VIVASVAN			SAVITR		BHRSA
DAU-VARIKA	JAYA						SAVITR	ANTA-RIKSA
PITARAH	MRGA	BHRN-GARAJA	GAN-DHARVA	YAMA	BRHAT-KSATA	VITATHA	PUSAN	ANILA

PAPARAKSASI   PILIPINJA   CARAKI

JAMBHAKA   SARVA-SKANDA

PUTANA   ARYAMAN   VIDARI

PLAN I: KAILASANATHA, KANCHIPURAM

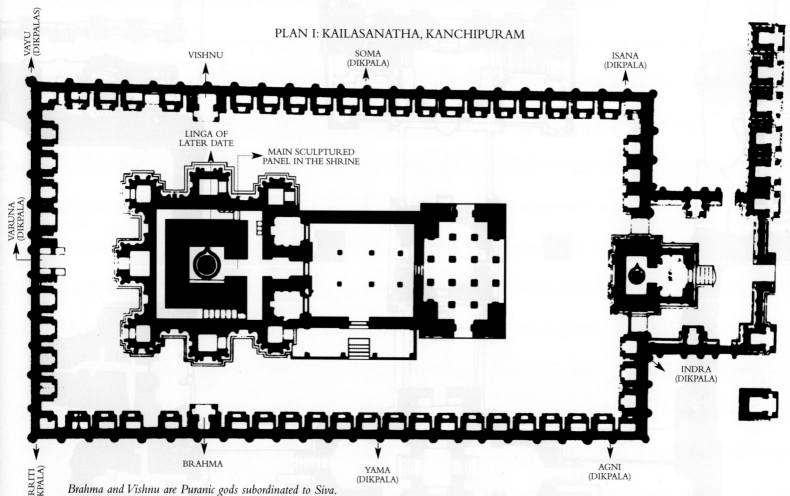

VAYU (DIKPALAS)

VISHNU   SOMA (DIKPALA)   ISANA (DIKPALA)

VARUNA (DIKPALA)

LINGA OF LATER DATE

MAIN SCULPTURED PANEL IN THE SHRINE

INDRA (DIKPALA)

NIRRITI (DIKPALA)   BRAHMA   YAMA (DIKPALA)   AGNI (DIKPALA)

Brahma and Vishnu are Puranic gods subordinated to Siva.

Chapter 2

The Temple: Its Cosmological and Metaphysical Origins

IN INDIA, COSMIC SYMBOLISM DOMINATES RELIGIOUS TRADITION and ideology which provides the focus for all spheres of human activity from birth to death and for social, economic and political organisation and institutional formations. The temple is the most significant of all these institutions, and hence, is conceived of as a cosmos in miniature, a replica of the cosmos, which brings alive the cosmic man *(purusha)*. The temple is built on a planned site called the *vastupurushamandala*. *Vastu* signifies residence and also means residue, literally meaning remainder (the extent of existence in its ordered state). *Vastu Sastra* is the science of architecture. The *vastupurushamandala* is a geometrical device or *yantra* *(yantr* – to bind) by which any aspect of the Supreme Principle may be bound to any spot for the purpose of worship. The cosmic man is believed to be identical to the planned site – the *vastumandala*. *Mandala* denotes a closed polygon. The essential form of the *vastupurushamandala* is a square, a stable form, which is the fundamental motif of Indian architecture. Among architectural symbols representing thoughts believed to be universal to mankind, the square and the circle are the most significant. The square is the archetype, and the pattern of order in the Indian tradition, as laid down in the *Brihat Samhita* (literally, the great collection), a compendium of the 5th century on various subjects including art and architecture. The Hindu temple also has the square as its essential form. Just as Mount Meru, the mythical mountain and axis of the universe according to Hindu belief, rises from a square base, the structure of the temple also rises from the square *vastupurushamandala*. Based on the square, the structure of the temple arises in the mid-world *(antariksha)* of air. It is built in three dimensions and of different substances: brick, wood or stone. As the perfect shape, the square is sacred in the hierarchy of architectural symbolism and is believed to contain the cycles of measurable time. It is followed by the circle, rarely used in temple architecture. These two symbols are considered to be the ornaments of *dharma,* the order of things in the cosmos, the square symbolising the world of gods, and the circle symbolising the world of man, exemplifying spiritual and temporal power respectively.

The square, as the fundamental figure of Vedic sacrificial symbolism and temple architecture, lends itself to many variations and still retains its symbolism. It can be converted into a triangle, hexagon, octagon and circle of equal area. The types of *vastumandala* are thus enumerated in a progressive series of squares, 64 and 81, and these numbers are prescribed for the temple of the Brahmana (priestly caste) and the temple and palace of the Kshatriya (ruling/warrior caste) respectively. Though this was not strictly followed even in the period of the most significant developments in

Facing page above: In the earliest known text Brihat Samhita, *the* Vastu *was the place of the adjustments of the solar and lunar cycles, for the placement of the deities. The 32 padadevatas (divinities) in the square borders, include the regents of the four quarters (cardinal points) and the 28* nakshatras *(stars). The* Brahmasthana *(the black square in the centre) is the place for the main deity. Here it is Brahma.*

Below: Plan of Kailasanatha temple, Kanchipuram, 7th century AD. It follows the Vastupurushamandala *in locating the central shrine in the* Brahmasthana *and the* padadevatas *in the peripheral shrines.*

13

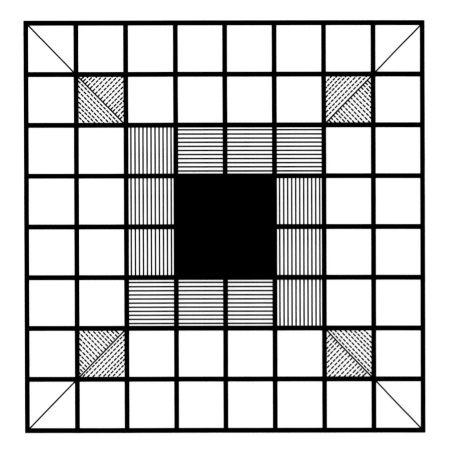

Vastumandala of 64 squares based on the Mayamata and Manasara, late medieval texts. The black square in the centre is the Brahmasthana, but Brahma is replaced by the Puranic Siva or Vishnu. The shaded squares are meant for the 32 divinities – the eight dikpalas and regents of the nakshatras/planets etc. located either in niches on the outer walls of the temple or in peripheral shrines in the enclosure wall, thus leaving an open space for circumambulation. See plan on p. 12 (Kailasanatha).

temple architecture under the most powerful ruling dynasties, this may have been accepted as the norm for the hierarchical order of buildings, in keeping with the stratified levels of social organisation based on the *varna-jati* concept, or the caste system of the Hindus. The temple as a place of worship and an institution was created by the ruling elite – the dominant social groups, the Brahmana and the Kshatriya, who enjoyed socio-political dominance over other castes.

The *vastumandala* or the square diagram of existence, measurable in space, is thus the metaphysical and cosmological plan of the temple and the temple's cosmological and magical implications are said to derive from it. The imaging of the cosmos is achieved by the presence of the planets, the stars, the guardians of the directions (32 divinities) who are accommodated on the border or perimeter of the *vastumandala*, with various other deities subsidiary to the main deity of the temple, who occupies the centre (the shrine) or the *Brahmasthana*. The *vastumandala* is the place of manifestation. The *Brahmasthana* is the vital centre, the place of realisation of the supreme Brahman, a place assigned to Brahma, Lord of Creation, in the Vedic tradition. In the Puranic tradition this position is assigned to the major Hindu gods, Vishnu and Siva, while Brahma becomes subordinated, although the concept of the Trinity – Brahma, Vishnu and Siva, as the Creator, Protector and Destroyer (of evil) respectively – continues in the Hindu tradition. Siva manifests himself as the *linga* (phallic symbol), while Vishnu manifests himself in his divine forms and incarnations (*avataras*). Both these deities are the Universal Brahman in their respective systems of belief and worship, while the other Vedic divinities remain in their position of subordination as *padadevatas* in the perimeter of the *vastumandala*. This cosmic symbolism is predominant in temples, which were royal projects and were built for legitimising the sovereignty of the respective rulers and intended as metaphors of royal authority.

The 32 divinities, known as the *padadevatas*, represent the gods of the Vedic pantheon and are assigned a subsidiary position in the *mandala* as regents of the stars (*nakshatras*) stationed on its border and led by the warders (*lokapalas*) of the four regions of space (Mahendra on the east, Yama on the south, Varuna on the west and Soma on the north) and guardians (*dikpalas*) of the cardinal and intermediate directions. The eight *dikpalas* are Indra, Agni, Yama, Niriti, Varuna, Marut, Kuvera and Isana. In the *Vastu* texts, the *yantra* symbolising cosmic order is the place of manifestation of the *vastupurusha,* whose various organs are equated with or presented in the form of the main deity in the centre and the other gods in the periphery. Its superstructure is the temple.

Understood correctly, the *vastumandala* is a prognostication for the building of a temple, and in a literal sense, the programme of the temple. The *vastupurushamandala*

– the temple-diagram and its metaphysical plan – is thus the intellectual foundation of the building, a forecast of its ascent, and its projection on the earth. This does not imply an identity of the actual plan of the temple with the *mandala*. The *mandala* is a prototype of the infinitely varied temple plans and the wide variety of designs that were developed in India in the making of the temple. It has immense potential in the process of the actual planning, designing and elaboration.

The drawing of the square *vastumandala* is a ritual pre-requisite to the making of a temple and, as every text on Indian architecture invariably lays down, it is an imperative prior to the building of a temple. However, the ritual and technical aspects of temple building are not easily distinguishable, for every movement in the drawing and execution of the plan is treated as a rite, knowledge of which the *sthapati* (mason) is expected to acquire and follow in a pre-ordained order. Thus the making of the Hindu temple from the planning of the site to the designing and execution of its shape, elevation,

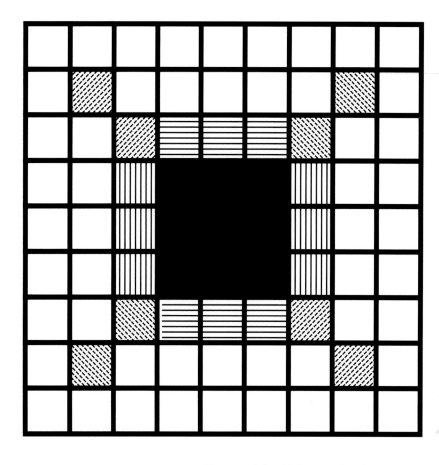

Vastumandala *of 81 squares based on the* Samaranaganasutradhara *and* Tantrasamucekaya. *The black square in the centre is the* Brahmasthana, *but Brahma is replaced by the Puranic Siva or Vishnu. The shaded squares are meant for the 32 divinities – the eight* dikpalas *(as found in the Kanchipuram and Tanjavur temples) are Indra, Agni, Yama, Niriti, Varuna, Vayu, Soma and Isana.*

carvings and iconographic programme is ritualised and its sanctity underlined. The ritual act and the actual process of building together go into the making of the temple. The ritual process includes the act of giving stability to the site, purification, insemination (the act of sowing seeds and their germination to signify the birth of a holy site) and levelling of the site; the diagram of the *mandala* marks the beginning of the construction. In the various phases in the construction and consecration of the temple, the rite of the seeds and their germination (*ankurarpana*) is the most important and precedes the building of the temple, and is observed again before the last brick is put into the superstructure, also prior to the installation of the main image and before the rite of opening the eyes of the image, and finally, prior to the consecration of the sacrificial vessels. The point of the final of the temple is an urn (*kalasa*). When the temple is completed and consecrated, its effigy, in the shape of a golden man, the *prasada-purusha*, is installed in a golden jar above the *garbha griha* (the shrine in which the deity is enshrined). After consecration, a large flag is fixed at the top.

The orientation of the temple follows the cosmic directions. Temples invariably face the east as it is the auspicious direction of the rising sun, whose first rays illuminate the interior of the shrine at dawn. There are exceptions in which Vishnu temples sometimes face the west or south depending upon the specific associations of a sacred centre. The sacred precinct is often demarcated by a surrounding wall enclosing an open space called the *prakara* (courtyard) within it. The main entrance gateway (*gopura*) to the temple precinct also thus comes to be located on the east, although entrances are built in all the four cardinal directions, with the addition of several enclosures to a temple. While canonical texts (*Agamas*) lay down rules regarding the orientation, layout and placement of various architectural features and iconographic forms, the science of architecture, *Vastu Sastra*, follows the canon and

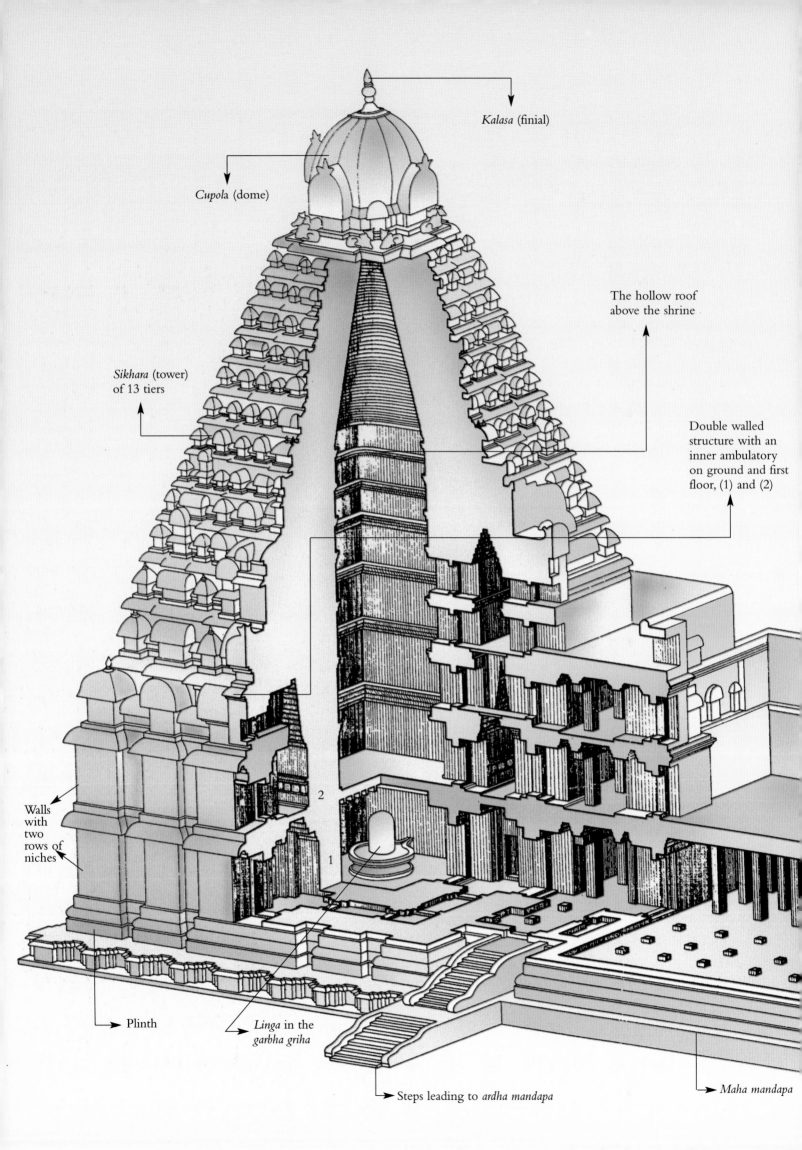

Kalasa (finial)

Cupola (dome)

The hollow roof
above the shrine

Sikhara (tower)
of 13 tiers

Double walled
structure with an
inner ambulatory
on ground and first
floor, (1) and (2)

Walls
with
two
rows of
niches

2

1

Plinth

Linga in the
garbha griha

Steps leading to *ardha mandapa*

Maha mandapa

lays down in detail the location of all the parts of a temple at appropriate places within the temple precincts. Cosmic structures are reflected in the location of various shrines within the temple, as the temple is conceived of as as a cosmos in miniature.

The position of the images are fixed in relation to the *vastumandala*. Theoretically the position of various temples within a settlement and also outside of it and in relation to it are also determined by cosmic orientation with reference to the sun, metaphysical orientation with reference to the centre of the *vastupurushamandala* and the centre of the settlement. Man being the living being (*jiva*), his welfare and peace are the considerations which are believed to determine where a temple faces.

Historical Origins

It is often believed that the temple form is derived from the Vedic altar, the earliest known sacred structure (*vedi*), which had the square as its essential form. However, many other origins are assigned to it with equal, perhaps greater, validity. Although from the Vedic altar to the Puranic (Hindu) temple, the square remains the essential form, the temple has no direct origin in the Vedic altar. Yet this is what many canonical texts and traditional writings on the temple attempt to establish, evidently to seek great antiquity and Vedic authenticity for the temple, which is the enduring symbol of Hindu culture. When the Vedic religion of sacrifice (*yajna*) gave place to the Puranic cults dominated by *bhakti* (devotion) and worship of personal deities like Vishnu and Siva, the temple became the focus of every sphere of human activity. The temple, unlike the Vedic altar, does not fulfil its purpose by being built; it is of necessity to be seen (*darsana*). Art enhances it and it becomes a holy site (*tirtha*). The purpose of visiting a temple was and still is to have a *darsana* of the temple, the seat, abode and body of divinity and to worship the divinity. Offerings and gifts (*dana*) have replaced the sacrificial tradition of old.

Apart from the square Vedic altar, other non-Vedic, non-metaphysical and more acceptable historical beginnings are assigned to the temple. For example, the present-day flat-roofed shrine is often seen as a derivation from an aboriginal prototype, the stone dolmen or a sepulchral structure which first appeared in the megalithic age in the centuries immediately before and after the beginning of the Christian era. The stone dolmen was a small chamber formed by

Perspective of the Tanjavur temple. Chola, 11th century. The temple consists of the vimana *(shrine with tower), a height of 63.41 metres from the base to the finial; and* ardha mandapa, maha mandapa *and* mukha mandapa. *The tower is of 13 tiers and the shrine is enclosed by double walls with space for an inner ambulatory on the ground and first floor. The plinth has two rows of niches for images.*

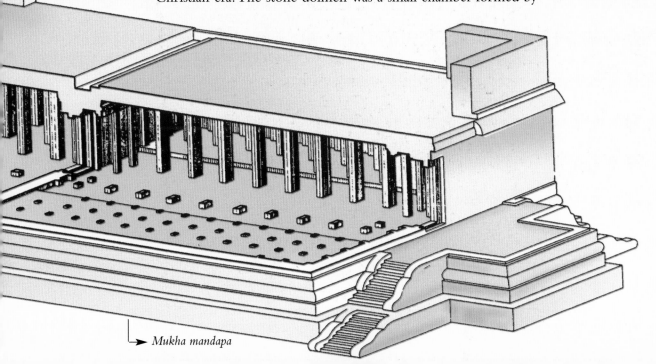

➤ *Mukha mandapa*

one large slab of stone, supported by three upright slabs set on their edges, with one side open to serve as an entrance. It could well have been the prototype of the early central Indian Gond temples and the flat-roofed central Indian and south Indian temples, like the ageless varieties of village and wayside shrines with their cubical walls covered by a flat roof, which can be seen even today. It is this cubical cell, which is transformed in the early medieval period (6th to 12th centuries) by being raised on a well-packed socle, and standing on a terrace in larger temples, and finally being embodied in the Hindu temple with its towering superstructure.

Another significant derivation of the temple was from the tabernacle of the forest, made of bamboo, or branches of large palm leaves only, in which a divine presence was known to dwell. The tabernacle, seen as an altar, enclosed the sacred space by the high shape of four curved branches with their ends gathered to a point in gradual reduction of the three dimensional form in one direction or in an ascent. This is still a familiar form in village huts. This form gave way to the curvilinear *sikhara* (superstructure) of the north Indian temple, ascending in diminishing units towards a finial, marked by the *kalasa,* a vase or an auspicious pitcher. Thus the four-sided, pyramidal or curvilinear superstructure predominated over other temple types, with flat or keel and barrel-shaped roofs.

Architectural Texts

The science of architecture, *Vastu Sastra* is treated as an *Upaveda* (subsidiary to the Vedas) in the *Brihat Samhita* of Varahamihira, which belongs to the period of the earliest extant temples – the Gupta period (4th–6th centuries). Several architectural texts were composed after the *Brihat Samhita* in the early medieval period. Of these, the 10th-century texts like the *Samaranaganasutradhara* of central India, the *Tantrasamucekaya* of south India, the *Aparajitapriccha* of western India are well known. The *Mayamata* and *Manasara* of the 17th–18th centuries are south Indian texts followed till this day. They represent the accumulated knowledge of centuries of a growing tradition.

Vastu Sastra texts, conventionally attributed to the divine architect of the universe, Visvakarman, but composed at various points of time from the 5th to 17th centuries, represent a growing tradition. They call the temple by different names. The temple is variously known in Sanskrit as the *prasada, vimana, devagriha,*

The sanctum, in the Siva temple, Halebid, Karnataka. The linga or the aniconic form is invariably enshrined in the sanctum. The bull (Nandi), his vehicle (vahana) is facing the shrine. Two doorkeepers (dvarpalas) flank the doorway with decorative lintel.

devayatana, devalaya and *mandiram. Prasada* and *vimana* are the most commonly used terms to refer to the main and integral part of the Hindu temple. The *vimana* (*ma*: to measure), proportionately measured throughout, is conceived of as the house and body of god. All other structures within the sacred precinct are accessory and subservient to it. They are usually aligned in an axial line with the *vimana* and conform in each case with its proportions. These include the *antarala* (vestibule) and *mandapas* (halls) for different purposes, mainly for ritual and congregational worship and performances of music and dance.

Prasada, the other name of the main building, is synonymous with *vimana*. According to the *Silparatna* (a *Vastu Sastra* text), '*prasadas* please by their beauty the minds of gods and men'. The term *prasada* is applied to many other buildings, some of which are *sabha* (assembly hall), *sala* (hall of learning), *prapa ranga mandapa* (hall for performances).

The main shrine symbolises, by means of its architecture, the universe, its manifestation and integration. It incorporates in its structure all the images. The pillar of the universe is believed to be inherent in it as the main shrine is believed to be the universe in its likeness. As the symbol of the world mountain, the *prasada* carries all the world's strata along its axis, which is the central pillar of the temple visible above its curvilinear superstructure, in the form of its neck (*griva*). The *amlaka* (ribbed myrobalan) and the *stupi* (finial) are the shapes and symbols of the vertical axis of the temple where it emerges into visibility. Thus, the finial extends into mid-space. The finial rises above the *harmya* (high temple). The *amlaka* above the *stupika*, the highest point, marks the limit between the unmanifest and the manifest. The hierarchy of divine manifestation is thus accommodated in the monument, located within its vertical axis, the cosmic pillar. The *kalasa* surmounting the top is the most important part as it is in this jar that the symbolic golden man (*prasada purusha*) is installed.

The Rangamahal cave, Ellora, Deccan, 8th century AD. The linga *in the sanctum* (garbha griha), *and the doorjambs with decorative panels representing the river goddesses, Ganga and Yamuna, are characteristic of the Gupta and post-Gupta temples of the* nagara *style in north India and the Deccan. The* dvarpalas *flank the shrine entrance.*

The Sikhara and its Types

The *sikhara* or the superstructure of the Hindu temple, first referred to in the texts known to us from the 5th–6th centuries, rises from the perpendicular walls of the *prasada* and covers the *garbha griha*. The curvilinear superstructure (*nagara sikhara*) is derived from the tabernacle of leaves, bamboo or branches curving towards one

A bronze image of Siva, the Lord of Dance, in the Chatura pose, different from the well-known Nataraja. Ellora, 8th century AD. The Chatura or square position of the legs is part of a dance movement (karana) described in Bharata's Natya Sastra, the 7th century treatise on dance.

point. This type of *sikhara* became the pre-eminent shape of the Hindu temple. The multiple proliferations of its shape may be seen in north India and the Deccan. The straight-edged pyramidal superstructure (*dravida sikhara*) is composed of storeys (*bhumis*), either a single storey or multiple storeys with tiers diminishing in size as the *sikhara* ascends. It is marked by string courses of miniature shrines – square, oblong and apsidal. This type is found in the high temple or *jati vimana* of south India.

The *nagara sikhara*, with its manifold range, occurring in four-fifths of the subcontinent, the southern limit being the river Krishna-Tungabhadra, far surpasses the *dravida sikhara* in number and in its intricate distinctive design. Its main varieties are distinguishable on the basis of the manner in which the clusters of shrines are organised as a composite *sikhara* – the central curvilinear *sikhara* is surrounded by clusters of miniature *sikharas*, half *sikharas* leaning against the chest (*uras*) of the main *sikhara*, and of each successive part of the *sikhara* and high-quarter *sikharas* at recesses and corners, and so on. Variations in this arrangement occur in central India, Rajasthan, Gujarat and Maharashtra.

Major temple styles listed and described in the *Vastu Sastra* texts are the *nagara*, *dravida* and *vesara*, of which the prime position is assigned to the *nagara* as the universal and leading style. Next in importance, stylistically and in spatial and temporal spread, is the *dravida* of south India. The *vesara* or *varata* is the mixed style of the Deccan and was still in an experimental stage when the 10th–11th century texts were composed and when temple architecture was at its climax. The Deccan was the main zone of the evolution of the *vesara* form with variations based on sub-regions and their dynastic predilections. The classification of the three styles, especially in the south Indian texts, shows that they are generally named after the various regional schools and classified according to their superstructures.

The *nagara*, *dravida* and the *vesara*, as classified in the south Indian architecture texts, have a universal value. Even as the great temples of south India were being built, norms and proportions were being laid down and styles classified in the architectural texts from the 10th century onwards, reflecting this growth and testifying to the changes or evolution. The south Indian texts focus on the *dravida prasada* and testify to the evolving differences between the early texts in the norms and proportionate measurements of the temple. In these texts lie the key to the complexities of the proportions of south Indian temples. *Ganyamana*, the proportionate vertical measurement of the height of the temple and of its component parts is elaborated in the south Indian *Vastu Sastra* texts. Sometimes entire chapters are devoted to the various components and their sub-divisions and proportions, such as the *adhishthana* (base). From the early nucleus of a shrine to the large temple complexes, both in their vertical and horizontal expansions, temple architecture represents a growing tradition. As distinct from the myriad patterns of the plan and rhythms of the walls and their surface decoration, which the north Indian method developed, the art of severe stereometry characterises south Indian architecture.

Sculpture

The Hindu temple is a monument, not of mere architectural virtuosity, but also a repository of works of sculpture, for the outer surface consists of statues of the various forms of the deity in what are called the *avarana koshthas* (surrounding niches). Thus the rite of circumambulation (*pradakshina*) by the devotee is more a communion by movement with the images in the niches of the walls than a visual recognition of their identity and the perfection of their workmanship. In fact, the temple is meant to be a monument for the manifestation of the divinity whose image or symbol is enshrined in the *garbha griha*, while the chief images (*parsvadevatas* or the main aspects of the divinity) are placed in the niches of the walls. Both ritually and iconographically, they are a part of the temple.

The temple is the stationary (*sthira/achala*) form, the chariot is the movable (*chala*) form of the house of god. The same distinction applies to the image – it is either immovable or *dhruvabhera*, permanently fixed in the shrine, or it is movable and carried about in procession. Bronze images of the deity are therefore an essential part of the ritual needs of the temple. The main deity in the shrine, made of stucco, wood or stone, is the *achala* or immovable, while the bronze images are the *chala* or movable (*utsava beras)* icons meant for worship through *abhisheka* (sacred bath), *alankara* (decoration) and *archana* (ritual offerings), and more importantly, through processions.

Apart from the main images in their niches, images of the *astadikpalas*, the guardians of the eight points of space, are given specific positions as laid down in the *Vastu Sastra*. Other divine and semi-divine mythical figures, stationed between these two kinds of essential images are *nagas* (serpents), *sardulas* (a hybrid of a lion and a bird), *apsaras* (celestial beauties representing female power), *mithunas* (amorous couples), all of whom denote fertility. Lesser gods are displayed on other parts of the temple structure, such as the base, the doorways, the *mandapa* ceiling or on pillars as *salabhanjikas* (bracket figures), and on *toranas* (free-standing gates). The threshold to the shrine is of particular significance as it is decorated with many auspicious features such as river goddesses, procreative couples and serpents on the doorjambs. As the threshold also represents the entry or initiation, Goddess Lakshmi, bathed by elephants, is carved as the central image on the lintel. It also has the full-blown lotus symbol.

Bronze images of Ganesa, Siva and Subrahmanya with consorts i.e. the Saiva pantheon. Bronze idols are used as processional images during festivals, the chala *or mobile form representing the* achala *or fixed images consecrated in the sanctum.*

The Architect-priest and the Craftsmen

The designing architect, the *sthapati*, is the foremost of the craftsmen. Others are the *sutragrahi*, *takshaka* and *vardhakin* – the surveyor, sculptor and builder-plasterer-painter respectively. These craftsmen carry out the instructions of the *sthapaka*, the architect-priest, who has the qualifications of an *acharya* and is usually a Brahmana. While the *sthapati*, as laid down in the important architectural texts, should be proficient in the various sciences such as mathematics, astronomy, astrology, prosody, philosophy and the arts, the *sthapaka*, who is the patron (*yajamana*) presents gold, clothes, ornaments to the mason according to his ability. In turn, the *sthapati* makes over a gift of gold to the *takshaka* and receives from him the entire merit for the work. The Indian craftsmen, it is generally believed, were anonymous. Many, however, signed their names like Narasobha in an Aihole (in Bijapur district in north Karnataka) inscription, as an expert in the art of building temples. Many are known only from the names of their patrons, whose titles are prefixed to the name of the artist who is only designated as *acharya*. In the temples of the Hoysalas, a ruling dynasty of south Karnataka between the 11th and 14th centuries, are found the most numerous references to the families of architects or masons who migrated in search of patronage. The artisans were remunerated for their services in the form of land and consumable items, apart from residential quarters.

Material and Method

The materials used for temple building, were and still remain, brick, wood and stone. From the 6th century, the time of the compilation of the earliest treatises on architecture, stone is one of the accepted materials. Whatever the material, the work was done with precision. No cementing material was used. Iron clamps were used for wooden joints. Where the masonry was dry, the stone blocks were held together with iron dowels (considered necessary). *Sudhasila* or plaster and *vajralepa* (literally diamond plaster, meaning strong plaster), a glue cement and coating were applied. The practice of building with cyclopean stones persisted in Hindu temples. Courses of dry masonry of carefully dressed and relatively very large stones are found in Gupta, Chalukya and Chola temples. Brick and stone were combined in the same building. The body could be of brick, the doorframe of stone, and the superstructure of brick and stone (medieval south Indian and Deccan temples). Varied combinations were adopted for reasons of added strength. Carving in plaster and also in terracotta (Bengal temples) was known. Trabeation and corbelling were employed in the *prasada* and the *mandapa* for spanning spaces and constructing domes.

Simple and elementary principles for eliminating stress and strain have been favoured in Hindu temples by calculation of weight and overload in relation to the size and height of the temple. The method of interlocking all the parts, vertical as well as horizontal, the application of mortice and tenon joinery devices, and the building of massive walls or cellular or basal supports prove that technological progress was achieved by the urge to infuse stability and aesthetic value to the temple.

Temple Ecology

According to Hindu mythology, Gods resided on mountains, on riversides, and in groves or forests. Hence the ecology of the temple is closely related to these zones. While a tree is associated with every temple, they vary according to the ecological locale of the temple. Leaves of the sacred tree, *vilva* or bael (associated with Lord Siva), and the *tulasi* or basil plant (for Vishnu) are used in worship. The riverine settlements had their temples on the banks of rivers near *ghats* (cemented banks), and sacred tanks were constructed within the temple enclosure for ritual purposes and ablutions. However the most significant and symbolic association of the temple is with the mountain. The Hindu temple is a synthesis of many symbols. Its ecology is closely linked to this symbolism. The mountain symbolism is one such, either in the physical location of a temple being on or near a hill, or in its metaphysical equation with the mountain. In the varieties of temples listed in the architectural texts of the 10th–11th centuries, the most remarkable are the Meru, Mandara and Kailasa (centre of the universe and mythical mountains), as they denoted the largest temples. Meru is said to be a mythical mountain of the greatest height. Hence, temples were classified in the architectural texts, according to Meru, according to their size, height and importance. The 32 Jatitara temples, mentioned in the texts of the southern school, are of different classes, hierarchically organised, starting from Meru. The Rajarajesvara temple at Tanjavur is named Dakshina Meru. According to myth, Meru is supposed to be the axis of the world. The mountain symbolism has many other associations such as the dark chamber or cavern/cave, mysterious and believed to house a secret (*rahasya*) as at Chidambaram in Tamil Nadu. The darkness of the chamber is a necessary condition for the transformation of the devotee, in whom a change is affected and a new life attained in the darkness of the shrine. The light swaying in front of the image creates a mystic luminiscence and inspires awe and reverence in the devotee. Cults associated with sacred mountains are numerous, and often in the past have determined the location of the temple and the town. The Tirumala-Venkatesvara temple in the wooded hills of the Eastern Ghats is now a famous

Sculptors (silpi) at work. The silpi and his assistants are trained in the traditional method of carving, the knowledge and technique being handed down from one generation to the next. Dhyana Slokas or memorised verses guide the sculptor in making the icon (in wood, stone and metal) with the iconographic attributes as laid down in the canon (Agamas), while the treatises on sculpture (Silpa Sastra) provide the technical details. The artist's freedom and skill are, however, reflected in the decorative aspects of the sculpture.

pilgrimage centre in Andhra Pradesh, but closer to the Tamil region and its cultural history. Tiruvannamalai in Tamil Nadu derives its sanctity from the steep rocky hills which rise to a height of 800 metres to its west. The hill is the visual focal point and the emblem of the place. Around it is organised the geographical, social and symbolic space of the town. The mountain also figures in the iconography and name of the deity, such as at Tiruvannamalai. The Arunachalesvara temple there is a substitute for the mountain which embodies Siva. The path for ritual circumambulation is ordered and oriented by the distribution, around a hill, of several shrines and ponds dedicated to the deities of the cardinal directions, punctuated by resting places and stations in the deities' processions. Such examples are fairly numerous and more conspicuous in south India. The idea of Mount Kailasa (located in the Himalayan range) as Siva's abode is often emphasised by the medieval practice of naming temples as Kailasa, and Siva as Kailasanatha, as at Ellora (Maharashtra) and Kanchipuram (Tamil Nadu) respectively.

The Siva temple, Tiruvannamalai, with its five enclosures built from 11th to 17th centuries AD with successive additions such as enclosures with mandapas and gateways of impressive size, expanding the temple horizontally. The temple derives its mountain symbolism from the local hill.

Chapter 3

Architectural Styles and Traditions: A Historical Perspective

INDIAN TEMPLE ARCHITECTURE EVOLVED FROM THE PERIOD OF the Gupta rulers (4th–6th centuries), who followed the Brahmanical religion and ideology and ruled from the present Allahabad (ancient Prayaga), at the confluence of the rivers Ganga, Yamuna and the lost Saraswati. Often characterised as the classical age in Indian art, the period witnessed two major developments. One was the maturity attained by the art of sculpture and the culmination of a sculptural tradition evolving from simple, archaic and static relief sculpture progressively transforming itself into a three-dimensional rounded and dynamic form, imbued with an inner spirit and strength and a sensitive portrayal of human, animal and floral devices. This was achieved initially by a conceptually and ideologically rich Buddhist tradition in the pre-Gupta period, and developed to its fullest capacity under the Brahmanical tradition in the Gupta and post-Gupta periods. The other was the formative phase of temple architecture, in which the principles and norms of erecting a temple were laid down, and gradually crystallised by the 6th century into two major temple styles – the *nagara* and the *dravida*.

Initially the temple originated as a flat-roofed square structure in the form of a cell (shrine) with a pillared porch in front. Variants of the flat-roofed structure persisted under the post-Gupta dynasties of north and central India, and the *nagara* style emerged with the evolution of a *sikhara* or superstructure over the square shrine. The subsequent development of the *nagara* style can be traced through regional schools, of which the major ones were those of Orissa (ancient Kalinga), central India (ancient Jejakabhukti-Mahoba), Rajasthan (the home of the Rajput dynasties) and Gujarat (ancient Gurjaradesa). These represent significant stylistic and aesthetic developments and variations in the vertical ascent and horizontal elaboration of the temple structure. In Uttar Pradesh (and its hill states), Bihar, Bengal and Himachal Pradesh, temples of the northern style were erected without architectural and stylistically significant differences. Kashmir developed a distinct class of temples away from the main *nagara* style.

The initial square and cubical form a simple square cell with a flat roof and a pillared veranda in front, as in Sanchi, Tigawa and Eran (central India) had great potential and later evolved into a wide variety of designs in different regions of north India, and were named after the respective regions. The brick and stone temples of the Gupta period show the development of the *sikhara* in the form of a straight-edged pyramid shaping into a curvilinear top surmounted by a cupola called the *amla sila*, a ribbed/cogged stone shaped like a myrobalan. The pyramidal tower is also marked by several tiers of architectural motifs, such as the *chaitya* (from

Facing page: Female bracket (madanika) figure, Kesava temple, Hoysala period (12th century). Belur, Karnataka. As decorative sculpture in the mandapa *ceilings and in the outer brackets at the cornice level, the beautiful female figures are used to enhance the aesthetic value of the monument and also as symbols of fertility and prosperity. In Orissa, Gujarat, Deccan and Karnataka they are depicted prominently.*

the Buddhist stupa shrine) and *amla*, the tiers diminishing in size as the tower ascends. Known as the *latina sikhara* (single turret), this is the basic design of all the *sikhara*s, which took the form of projections and recessions, the larger ones with a vertical ascent of an impressive array of such decorations, sometimes introducing miniature *sikhara*s at various points and levels of the tower. The most mature of the Gupta temples is that in Deogarh, Uttar Pradesh, which is a typical *latina sikhara* with other characteristic features.

The development of the *dravida* style was mainly confined to the region south of the Krishna river (south India), where the most significant progress took place from the 6th–17th centuries, in an almost unceasing architectural activity under the royal dynasties of the Pallavas and Pandyas (6th–9th centuries) and the Cholas (9th–13th centuries), followed by the Vijayanagara period (14th–17th centuries). The stylistic and technological progress is marked by the vertical ascent of the main shrine (*vimana*) from the 7th to the 11th centuries, and the horizontal magnification of the temple precincts in the form of huge pillared halls and enclosures with towering entrance gateways called *gopuras*, from the 12th century onwards. Thus emerged huge temple structures and temple towns in south India in places of sacred, political and economic importance due to continuous building activity under royal patronage, and community participation in temple building. While royal sponsorship and patronage in temple building activity arose out of the legitimate role of the temple, community participation was the result of the temple's importance as an integrative institution organising the social, economic and cultural life of the people. The expansion of the temple complex represents the gradual integration of various socio-economic, tribal-ethnic groups into temple society, making the temple the reference point for the enhancement of social status through rituals, economic progress and political influence.

The geographical distribution of the two styles is thus clearly marked as north and south Indian. However, the Deccan region of peninsular India is distinguished by an initial architectural evolution marked by features of both the styles from the 6th to 9th centuries, and subsequently, by what may be described as a hybrid style representing a mixture of the two, often identified as the third style of temple architecture called the *vesara*. In many ways the Deccan (now Maharashtra and Karnataka) and the Andhra region represent an intermediate zone in architectural development leading to a highly florid architectural design in the Chalukya (north and central Karnataka), Hoysala (south Karnataka) and Kakatiya (Hyderabad, Warangal and adjacent areas) temples of the 10th to 13th centuries.

The differences between the *nagara* and the *dravida* styles lie in the *vimana* design, the base and walls of the shrine exhibiting variations in mouldings, projections and recessions, with niches placed in prominent positions, and also in their decorative motifs. More significantly, the superstructure/tower is conceived of as a curvilinear roof in the *nagara* temple, while it is a storeyed/tiered construction marked by string courses of miniature shrines in the straight-edged pyramidal *dravida* style. Both, however, are erected on the principle of diminishing squares, the roof being hollow inside, which is hence described as a nest (*kudu*) in the *dravida* style. In both types of *vimana,* the close parallel or comparison with the human body is brought out by the description of the base as feet (*pada*), the walls as the body and limbs (*bhitti*), the position above the walls marked by a cornice as the neck (*griva*) and the roof as the head (*sikhara*). The symbolism is further emphasised by the whole shrine being described as the womb house (*garbha griha*) in which the deity is placed.

Schools of the Northern Nagara Style

■ *The Kalinga Style of Orissa:* It is in the regional schools that the evolutionary stages or the progression of the *nagara* style can be traced. The evolution and meridien of the style are illustrated in the Kalinga region during the 7th to 13th centuries. This was the period in which several small sub-regions, ruled by minor lineages came to be integrated into a single politico-cultural region called Kalinga (now Orissa), under a powerful regional dynasty of early medieval India called the Eastern Gangas. Iconographically rich, these temples have works of sculpture in their niches representing various forms and manifestations of the deities to whom the temples are dedicated.

The Kalinga style, particularly its *sikhara*, may be derived from Gupta architecture. Even the earliest Orissa *sikhara* is a fully evolved graceful structure in which the various storeys have been fused into one continuous outline. This regional school passed through several phases of development, the earliest represented by the temples of Mukhalingam (7th century) in the southern part of Orissa. The architectural movement, however, gained momentum in the temples of Bhubaneswar, the Parasuramesvara temple (AD 650) and its cognate group of the 7th–9th centuries, marking the beginning of a long process of development till the 13th century. This phase is marked by a simple curvilinear tower over the square sanctum, a hall (*mandapa*) called the *jagmohana*, with a flat roof, but with a clerestory above the plain pillarless (*astylar*) hall, devoid of any interior decorations. On the contrary, the exterior wall surfaces are more profusely decorated. The early temples have no socles to accentuate their elevation. Later and bigger temples are accentuated by a socle or base and by the verticality of the tower.

The two main parts of the Kalinga temple – the *rekha deul* (shrine or *sri mandir*) and the *pidha deul* (hall or *jagmohana*) are gradually elaborated in an axial alignment by the addition of a *nritya mandapa* (hall for dance) and a *bhoga mandir* (hall of offerings), in examples where the meridien of the Kalinga style has been reached. This is evident in the 11th century Lingaraja temple in Bhubaneswar. The temple here is a work of monumental sculpture of which simple carvings form the intricate surface. The curvilinear and the pyramidal are here used conjointly for the *rekha deul* and the *pidha deul* (shrine and hall).

Kalinga's architectural experiments resulted in several interesting designs. The *vaital deul*, which is a *panchayatana* temple (a temple with five shrines), has an oblong shrine in the place of the square one with a new type of roof – a vaulted wagon-topped *sikhara* with foliated gable ends. This is comparable to the apsidal Buddhist *chaitya* and later *gopura* entrance of the *dravida* temples. The Ananta Vasudeva temple, also a *panchayatana*, retaining the square plan and the curvilinear *sikhara*, is more fully evolved, taller, with additions such as the *nata* and *bhoga mandirs*, and is a proto-type of the 11th-century Lingaraja temple. The Lingaraja marks the apogee of the *nagara sikhara*, while the Jagannatha temple at Puri and the sun temple at Konarak mark the grandeur of its style.

Siva as Ravananugrahamurti. According to legend, Ravana, the demon king, the anti-hero of the epic Ramayana, *became an ardent devotee of Siva after his vanity was subdued by him. When Ravana tried to display his strength by lifting the Kailasa mountain on which Siva dwelt with his consort Parvati, Siva pressed the mountain down with his toe. Here, Ravana's figure is more prominently sculpted, in an aesthetically pleasing posture (as if dancing), holding the mountain with one of his 20 hands. Ravana was a ten-headed asura (demon). This theme is popular in Ellora and other Deccan sites as also in the sculpture and paintings of the Chola temples.*

A more ornate example is the Muktesvara, also in Bhubaneswar, which has a decorative free-standing gateway in addition to the two main parts of the temple and an aesthetically better elevational design. With its interior decorations, hitherto not known, it takes the style onwards to its high point in the 11th century. A new maturity and superior craftsmanship are evident in its work of sculpture, both in the icons and decorative figures of the celestial nymphs (*alasa kanyas*) and serpent forms (*nagas* and *nagins*). It is aptly described as a miniature gem of architecture.

The Rajaraniya is a unique experiment with the earliest *sikhara* of multiple turrets or *urah sringas* in high relief attached to the main *sikhara* at various points. Standing on a base heightening its elevation, this temple is the forerunner of the massive, multi-turreted *sikharas* of the *nagara* style at Khajuraho and its variants in Rajasthan and Gujarat. The Kalinga school, however, did not carry this experiment to its logical conclusion, and hence, stuck to its *rekha sikhara* with an occasional miniature shrine on the corners of the main shrine as in the Lingaraja and Jagannatha temples. This school not only evolved the four components of the temple, but also an enclosure with an entrance gateway, rarely found in northern *nagara* schools of architecture. The Lingaraja illustrates this complete plan and design. Its quadrangular enclosure measures 158.5 x 142 metres. The temple at Puri (AD 1118) is a replica of the

The Siva temple of Lingaraja, Bhubaneswar, 11th century AD. The large temple complex is dominated by the main shrine with its rekha or *curvilinear tower and the* jagmohana *(hall of worship) with its pyramidal tower. Several subsidiary shrines within the huge enclosure also have the* rekha sikhara *(tower). The Kalinga (Orissa) school of the* nagara *temple architecture reached its apogee in this temple.*

Lingaraja, but on a larger scale with more impressive proportions and two enclosures, the whole measuring 203 x 195 metres. It stands on an eminence soaring in height as the tower is 61 metres high. This temple underwent later additions and renovations.

Experiments continued in the largest and most impressive temple – the sun temple at Konarak, which remained either incomplete or was too ambitious to stand the ravages of time, but still preserves some novel ideas in design and decoration. The sun temple at Konarak is in a class by itself, representing the most ambitious project of the Eastern Gangas, who planned a much larger structure, consisting of the main shrine and the *jagmohana* in one unit, in front of which they designed a separate and fair-sized hall (*nata mandir*); the whole series of structures was surrounded by a courtyard with an entrance. Abul Fazl, the Mughal chronicler of Akbar's court, eulogises about it in his *Ain-i-Akbari*, saying, 'Even those whose judgement is critical and who are difficult to please stand amazed at the sight.' The large courtyard measures

Torana, free-standing gateway, Muktesvara temple, Bhubaneswar, 8th century AD. The torana is an unusual architectural feature found in the Kalinga (Orissa) and Maru-Gurjara (Gujarat and Rajasthan) schools of nagara *architecture. The Muktesvara is a gem amomg the temples of Orissa.*

Facing page: *The Sun temple, Konarak, Orissa. 13th century AD. The tower of the sanctum is either lost or could never be built due to the ambitious plan and design of the temple. Here, the* jagmohana *with its pyramidal tower is built in the form of a chariot on wheels drawn by the seven horses of the sun. The wheels are remarkable for their minute carvings including erotic sculpture. Chariot-like* mandapas *are also known in some Siva temples in Tamil Nadu.*

264 x 165 metres. Much of this complex has disappeared or was never completed, but what remains is sufficient proof of the magnitude and unique design of the temple. Its *jagmohana* was conceived of in the form of a chariot on wheels drawn by seven horses, the wheels being richly carved with figural and other decorative motifs, erotic figures being prominent among them. The superstructure of the *jagmohana* survives with its stepped up tiers carrying bold life-size statues of dancers and musicians. Sun temples are not usually rich in icons, for there is no separate pantheon which evolved around this deity, except for his attendants, consorts and charioteer, Aruna. This is more than compensated by the decorative carvings, which are among the most remarkable in temple sculpture in India. Ruined and abandoned due to ravages of time and the decline of formal sun worship as part of the mainstream religious system of the Hindus, this temple on the sea-shore is more a tourist attraction today, except once in a year when pilgrims from neighbouring regions and from distant places visit the temple to worship the sun god.

No significant architectural development is noticeable after the 13th century, yet the textual tradition in Orissa was crystallised and canonised in the medieval period. By the 17th century, the most remarkable text, the *Silpaprakasa,* came to be written, providing the grammar and key to the understanding of temple architecture in Orissa. The *Silpaprakasa* and the *Bhuvanapradipa* are two texts which have preserved different versions and accumulated knowledge of the architectural traditions of Orissa, developing their own nomenclature.

In the iconographic scheme in the Orissan temples, the walls of the shrine are divided into three vertical segments with a large niche in the centre of each wall housing a *parsvadevata.* In a Siva temple, these niches house the images of Parvati and her two sons Ganesa and Kartikeya; in a Vishnu temple we find the three forms of Vishnu; in a Devi temple there are the three forms of the goddess. The *parsvadevata* niche is flanked by smaller niches containing the relief statues of the deity to whom the temple is dedicated. The Gupta formula of introducing the figures of the river goddesses Ganga and Yamuna with their vehicles (the tortoise and crocodile, respectively) on the doorjambs of the shrine was invariably followed. From rigid, frontal forms, Orissa's stone sculpture changed and achieved, in a short span of time, a fluency and maturity of style.

The temples of Orissa are distributed all over the region, but the greatest concentration of historically and architecturally significant temples occurs in the Bhubaneswar-Puri-Konarak triangle. Bhubaneswar is the most important example of the evolution of the regional style. Puri became the focal point of the Jagannatha (Vishnu) cult in the 13th century when the integration of the sub-regions of Kalinga, originally controlled by minor ruling families, was achieved by the more powerful Sailodbhavas. In their political centre, Bhubaneswar, the largest number of temples came to be built between the 7th and 12th centuries. The final unification was brought about by the Eastern Gangas, contemporaries of the powerful south Indian dynasty, the Cholas. They were instrumental in establishing the cult of Jagannatha, representing the assimilation of three tribal deities into the Vaishnava religion and their transformation into the three Vaishnava deities, Balarama, Vasudeva and Subhadra. Krishna-Vasudeva later became Jagannatha (Lord of the World) and Purushottama (The Greatest Being). Henceforth, temples came to be erected all over the region for Jagannatha, big and small, but not of the same magnificence and

Temples at Khajuraho are notable for their highly decorative towers and mandapas of nagara architecture. The variegated pattern of the sikharas with miniature shrines on the tower and the mandapas with domical roofs and balconies create a rich interplay of light and shade. The high plinths on which the temples stand enhance their height.
Below: *Siva as Bhairava, Lakshmana temple. Khajuraho, 11th century AD. Bhairava is a malevolent aspect of Siva, who cut off Brahma's head and according to legend, had to atone for the sin of Brahmahatya (killing Brahma) by begging in the form of a naked ascetic, called Bhikshatana. A popular theme in south Indian iconography.*

architectural grandeur as the Puri temple, which was the royal temple, symbolising power and legitimising temporal authority. The Gajapati rulers of the 14th–15th centuries styled themselves as the servants of Jagannatha, by instituting festivals and performing the *cheropahara* ritual (the sweeping of the temple chariot or *ratha* during the chariot festival), when an image of Lord Jagannatha is taken out in procession in the huge temple chariot (*ratha yatra*). The *ratha* is the mobile (*chala*) form of the immobile (*sthira*) temple.

■ ***The Central Indian School – Khajuraho:*** Khajuraho (ancient Kharjuravahaka), located in present Madhya Pradesh, was originally a tribal region belonging to the Gonds. Here, the process of Sanskritisation must have been complete by the time its temples were built and the Puranic religion established. The Chandellas, who were worshippers of Maniya Deva, the deity of the Bhars (a Gond tribe), introduced the Puranic ideology both by claiming descent from the Chandravamsis (a royal race tracing its descent from the moon) and by adopting Puranic forms of worship.

The second major school of the *nagara* style was developed under the Chandellas of Jejakabhukti, who ruled from Khajuraho, a medieval city with a large number of Brahmanical temples dedicated to the Puranic gods, Siva and Vishnu, apart from a few Jain temples. Carefully planned and designed to enhance the monumental and architectural significance of the temple, the Khajuraho group of temples is famous for its grandeur and aesthetic appeal. Built during the 10th–12th centuries, these temples surround a lake of impressive size called the Sivasagar, and were described by Ibn Batuta (an Arab traveller) in the 14th century in his travelogue, *Rihlah*.

Of the legendary 85 temples, only 25 have survived and belong to three religions, Vaishnava, Saiva and Jain. Here, the shrine and the *mandapas* of a temple have trabeate domes of varying height. The tower of the Khajuraho temples adds to the visual impact of the superstructure by introducing miniature *sikharas* called *urah sringas* at every stage of the rising tower, that is, in the corners of the projections, thereby making the central Indian tower the most remarkable of all the *nagara* types of *vimanas*. The additional circumambulatory path around the main shrine, and the

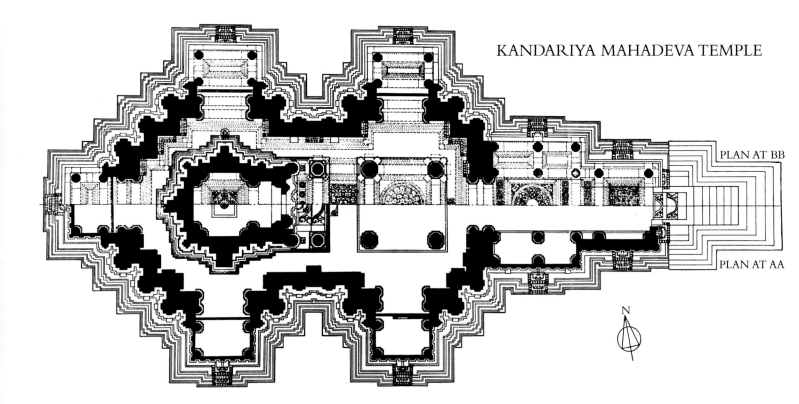

KANDARIYA MAHADEVA TEMPLE

PLAN AT BB

PLAN AT AA

N

Above: Plan of the Kandariya Mahadeva temple, Khajuraho. The four parts of the temple are the shrine, two pillared halls and an entrance porch. The projections and recessions from the base to the cornice or neck from which the towers begin, make an interesting pattern of vertical elevation, while friezes of sculpture at various levels bind the whole structure together horizontally.

Facing page: Figures in different erotic postures creating patterns on the kapili or junction of the shrine and mandapa of a Khajuraho temple. Khajuraho is unjustly famous for its erotic sculpture which comprises only ten per cent of the total and 90 per cent represents religious imagery.

second path surrounding the whole structure, with its balconies creating voids along the enclosing walls, enhance the interplay of light and shade on the temple's elevation. The base (*adhishthana*) is a high plinth with a running series of decorative friezes or bands representing elephants, horses and human forms. Above this base, on the walls, are prominent niche images and other figural statues. The erotic figures placed in the junction between the shrine and the *mandapa* form part of such sculptural decoration. The *sikhara* rises above this wall with its multiple miniature shrines creating the appearance of a massive mountain, the mountain symbolism being constantly emphasised in temple architecture. Standing on a heightened base, the whole temple dominates the landscape by its height and admirably balanced design.

It is in Khajuraho that the temple as the monument of manifestation comes alive in the two large temples of Lakshmana and Kandariya Mahadeva dedicated to Vishnu as Vaikuntha, and Siva as Sadasiva, respectively. They symbolise the cosmic and mythical Mount Meru and Kailasa, their towers rising like mountains with miniature *sikharas* graded and harmoniously arranged in proportionate and progressive ascent around the main *sikhara*. Both the temples express a unique sense of rhythm and are compact unified structures, erected in an east-west axis, each consisting of a *garbha griha,* an interior shrine or *antarala,* a closed hall or *gudha mandapa,* and a porch or *mukha mandapa .*

Each temple is a universe in itself, and this is how the major temples of the 11th–12th centuries have been conceived and erected. The Kandariya Mahadeva is a well-structured monument like a three-dimensional *mandala*, and is much more than the sum of its architecture and sculpture. It is alive with the manifestation of Siva surrounding the central *linga*. The cosmic symbolism is established by the presence of the *dikpalas, navagrahas* and other deities in the periphery of the *mandala*.

Fertility symbolism is inherent in the female figures of *apsaras, surasundaris,* and particularly the erotic figures on the junction walls, speaking a twilight (*sandhya* or dusk symbolising a threshold which is neither here or there*)* language (*bhasha*). These, and even the hybrid animal figures (*vyala*) possess an auspicious character and are believed to perform a magico-protective function.

Khajuraho has erroneously become synonymous with erotic sculpture, which, in fact, comprises only one-tenth of its imagery. It belongs to a different tradition, as do other medieval temple centres, where both religious and worldly interests merge. It is in the placement of the divinities and their configuration in the architectural scheme that the key to a proper understanding of the monuments lies. The erotic figures occur on the *kapili* or portion of the junction wall joining the sanctum and the hall, and convey something beyond the erotic – an intermediate zone or passage from this mundane world to the other, the higher and the spiritual. As temples of manifestation, the chief deities emerge from the unmanifest to the manifest, a process, which is visually represented through the various forms of Siva or Vishnu, in a graded hierarchy. The temple's pantheon progresses in surrounding niches (*avarana*) on the main walls of the temple, which the devotee passes to reach the ultimate deity enshrined in the *garbha griha.* The ranked hierarchy of the Puranic pantheon is also established – in the Siva temple, deities like Vishnu and Brahma are placed in a subordinate position, as also other celestial beings such as the *vidyadharas, gandharvas, apsaras, surasundaris, dikpalas,* hybrid animal forms like the *vyala,* decorative designs and many more. Thus, while cosmic symbolism characterises all major temples of the 11th–12th centuries in India, Khajuraho's design surpasses others in the order of the hierarchy of its miniature shrines and religious imagery.

Khajuraho, in fact, reflects the milieu and ambience of the Chandella court, as described in the *Prabandhachandrodaya* of Krishna Misra, the court poet, whose work is a philosophical allegory shedding authentic light on the religious environment of Khajuraho. Khajuraho shows the interface between art and politics, and art and literature, for the sculptors were well-versed not only in art, architecture and poetics, but also in the religious system of the temple, in which they were guided by the *acharya.*

■ *Temples of Gujarat, Rajasthan and Madhya Pradesh:* Temples of the *nagara* style were also built in the regions now represented by Gujarat, Rajasthan and western parts of Madhya Pradesh, once called Gurjaradesa, within which were several sub-regions ruled by different Rajput dynasties. (Maru *mandala* denoted the regions of Marwar, Sapadalaksha, Mewar and Bharatpur; Gurjara *mandala* consisted of Saurashtra, Kutch, and lower Rajasthan.) Groups of temples representing sub-regional styles were built during the 7th–9th centuries, when the Rajput dynasties rose to power and sought legitimacy through Brahmanical religious ideology or the Puranic religion. All these groups belonged to the generic *nagara* style, but are variants of it, as they evolved distinctive patterns of architectural design and decorative features. Basically, there existed three sub-regional schools, which are distinguishable by the forms of their *sikharas* and decorative elements. In fact, it would be extremely difficult to isolate the styles and their corresponding regions as there was considerable overlap in political authority and movement of ideas and

37

The octagonal pillared pavilion, Sun temple, Modhera Gujarat, Maru-Gurjara style. The pillars placed octagonally are highly decorative with minute carvings, figural sculpture and brackets with vandana-malikas (garland-like arches) connecting the pillars at the ceiling level.
Below: Entrance to the octagonal mandapa. The entrance pillars are linked by a vandana-malika.

stylistic features. Hence, the sub-regional varieties occur in many centres, marking the culmination of architectural development in this whole region of which Osia in Rajasthan has temples highlighting the different phases of the sub-regional styles, and also the genesis of the Maru-Gurjara style. The Maha-Maru style reached its zenith at Osia and Mandor and the Maha-Gurjara at Roda and Shamalaji by the 10th century. However, constant political changes, movement of trade, artisans and art traditions and patrons from different regions, led to the unification of these two styles into the Maru-Gurjara by the 11th–12th century. A third sub-variety of temples in the Malava region (western Madhya Pradesh) is classified as Bhumija temples, a distinctive Maru-Gurjara style, with its noble and virile form of superstructure, also seen at the Udayesvara temple at Udaipur (Rajasthan).

The mature Maru-Gurjara style is a distinctive expression of Indian temple architecture with very characteristic features. The temple does not stand on a socle or terrace (*jagati*). It consists of two structural parts, first, the main shrine (*mula prasada*) with a single turret (*latina sikhara*) or multi-turreted (*sekhari*) superstructure. The second is the closed hall (*gudha mandapa*) or a semi-open hall called *ranga mandapa* or *nritya mandapa*, meant for performances. These two are linked by a buffer wall called the *kapili* (juncture). Occasionally shrines (*bhadraprasada*) attached to the transcepts of a common hall are added. Sometimes a group of three shrines also occur on the cardinal offsets of the *ranga mandapa*. The temples are either with an inner ambulatory (*sandhara*) or without it (*nirandhara*). Later, in Jain temples, a four-faced entry plan or a *chaturmukha* arrangement was introduced, adding to the richness of the architectural design.

The orthogonal plan of the main shrine has either a single projection of the sides or two, three and four projections. Such a design enhances the aesthetic impact of the shrine, for these projections were carried right upto the end of the rising spire with turrets at every stage. Hence, the elevation of the shrine represents an integral whole of the socle (*pitha*), the wall (*mandovara*) and the spire (*sikhara*), above which are the usual neck (*griva*), myrobalan (*amla sila*) and pitcher (*kalasa*).

Among the 38 available *vastu* codes of the Maru-Gurjara architecture, the most important are the *Aparajitapriccha*, written under the Solankis, in whose period (11th–12th centuries), the development of the style reached its apogee, and the 11th-century *Samaranaganasutradhara*, authored by Bhoja, a Paramara ruler of Malava (1035–1055).

Gujarat: In the Solanki temples of Gujarat, the architectural scheme of the shrine and the *mandapa* is divided into three main sections, consisting of the base or *pitha*, the wall-face upto the entablature or cornice (*mandovara)*, and the superstructure, which is the spire or *sikhara*. The base is composed of a series of mouldings and string courses, the lowest being the horned heads (*rakshasa*); over this are the elephant forms or *gajapitha*, then come the horses or *asvathara*, and finally at the top are the human forms or *narathara*. The wall surface is exclusively meant for figure sculpture, with niches and tabernacles enshrining bas-relief images of the deities and other spiritual beings, mainly the pantheon.

The *sikhara* of the western temples have a distinctive treatment, as the spire is no longer one simple member, its lower portion being surrounded by a system of turrets or *urah sringas*. They are symmetrically arranged, each a replica of the large central structure, and each in such high relief as to be semi-detached or almost in the round. The *mandapa* has similar mouldings, but it is in its interior arrangement, its pillars and sloping seat backs (*kakshasana*) as well as the ceiling decorations that a spectacular vision is presented with the interplay of lavishly carved slender columns, bracket figures, floral garlands (*vandana malikas*) like *toranas* between the ceilings (*vitanas*) of unequalled beauty. The pillars have square or octagonal bases, 16-sided middle sections and circular tops. The centre of the *mandapa* is often an octagon around which the pillars are placed. The *mandapa* is covered by a roof built in the manner of a low pyramid (*samvarana*), with a series of bells marking the stepped-up pyramidal roof, diminishing in size and terminating in the usual vase-shaped finial. The *mandapa* interior being peristylar with elegantly carved pillars, its richly sculptured stratification and ceiling carvings contrasts with the innermost passage and chambers, which devoid of any decoration. The doorway (*dvarasakha*) to the sanctum is richly carved – the jambs and the lintel in particular. The central niche on the lintel often carries the image of the main deity or of Ganesa.

Architectural decoration, innovation and intricate devices, carried to extremes in the *ranga mandapa* of the Tejapala Jain temple at Dilwara, marked the zenith of the Maru-Gurjara style. Further developments took the form of more intricate and minute carvings on all available spaces of the temple structure, often described, not altogether appropriately, as the baroque in Indian art. This is a more pronounced characteristic of the post-Solanki temples, the Jain temples in particular, such as those on the Satrunjaya hill near Palitana and Girnar near Junagadh, dating upto the 17th–18th centuries.

The Solanki kingdom, with its rich traders and royal patrons, was able to finance ambitious and colossal projects like the Rudramahalaya at Sidhpur, the famous Somanatha at Prabhas Patan (several times restored in medieval times and rebuilt in the post-Independence era) and the Ajitanatha (Jain) temple at Taranga. Of the 10th–11th century temples in Gujarat and Kathiawar, the Surya temple at Modhera (1026–27) in Gujarat, though in ruins, has preserved the complete, well-evolved plan and design of this style. In addition, it has an ornamental tank (*kunda*) for ablutions, with a rectangular arrangement of terraces interspersed with shrines of various sizes and shapes, all admirably laid out. A flight of steps leads to an exquisitely carved and fluted archway to the main entrance of the temple.

Siva temple, Menal, Rajasthan. (11th–12th century). Schematic vertical rows of miniature shrines (uru-sringas) decorate the tower of the shrine. The tiered pyramidal tower of the square mandapa *in front of the shrine is called the* samvarana *because of the rows of bell-shaped motifs on the roof and provides an interesting foil to the tall tower.*

Rajasthan: In Rajasthan, temple-building activities were not extensive except in the less arid zones, such as Marwar and Jaipur regions. The Aravalli range of low hills (Sirohi, Abu, Udaipur, Chittor, Dungarpur, Banswara and Alwar states), with its ravines, valleys and water streams, provided shelter and security to many early Rajput ruling families. The Hadoti plateau and the eastern plains (Bundi, Kota and Jalawar states), more fertile on account of rivers like the Chambal, Bans, Mahi and their tributaries, have temples at Badoli, Chandravati on the Chandrabhaga, and even in remote areas.

The Puranic religions of Vaishnavism and Saivism being the two main religious traditions in Rajasthan, as in other regions of India in the early medieval period, temples of Siva and Vishnu were more numerous, while in some parts the worship of the sun and Sakti (Goddess of Power) was also in vogue and temples were built for these deities. Later, the sun cult was merged in the Vaishnava religion. The

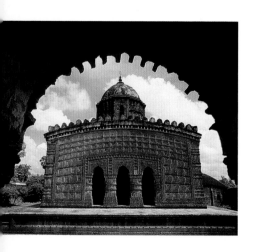

Madanmohan temple, Vishnupur, West Bengal. Brick temples with terracotta sculpture characterise Bengal temples of the 17th–18th centuries AD, which are described as the monumentalisation of dwelling huts. Islamic architectural influence is seen in the superstructures of these temples.

Pasupata cult was specially dominant in Kota, Jalawar, Sikar, Paranagar and Bharatpur. As in other regions of India, the *panchayatana* cult of the five deities – Vishnu, Siva, Surya, Sakti and Ganesa – was prevalent. Due to cult synthesis, Rajasthan abounds in syncretic representations of Vishnu-Surya (Suryanarayana), Vishnu-Siva (Harihara), Siva-Surya (Martanda-Bhairava) and Trimurti (a combination of Vishnu, Siva and Brahma) with Surya. Jalawar in Chandraprabha and Kota in Udaipur were strongholds of Sakti worship, as seen in their Navadurga temples.

As a political region, Rajasthan was never unified under a single powerful dynasty, and Rajput chieftains established themselves in different pockets of resource bearing and trading areas as their patrimonies. Their tribal and family affiliations continued even after such political regions emerged, and this is reflected in the temples built by these rulers. These legitimised the ruler's authority and were symbols of power and patronage. In the process of temple building not only were royalty and nobility involved, but also ministers (Jain), merchant princes under the Chahamanas, Paramaras, and particularly under the Solankis. Patronage to temples came also from merchants and bankers from Karnataka, Madhyadesa, Lata and Takkadesa. They built pavilions and arranged for *goshtikas* (organised groups) amongst them to be entrusted with the management of temples. Saiva *acharyas* were also made responsible for the building and maintenance of temples.

■ ***Bengal, Temples of Brick and Terracotta:*** Bengal followed the *nagara* style, particularly the *latina sikhara*, which evolved from the Gupta and post-Gupta temples of north India. However, no stone temple has survived in its entirety for a clear Bengal type to be identified. Yet, it is certain that this region's architecture developed in tandem with the main *nagara* style of north India. Most of the early medieval temples of Bengal are modest specimens built under the royal patronage of the Palas and Senas (8th–12th centuries), and had no significant contribution to make to the myriad forms of the *nagara* that developed in other major regions of north India. In Bahulara near Bankura, and Chandrakona in West Bengal, are remains of monumental buildings with the *rekha* type of north Indian *sikhara*, indicating the influence of the Orissa school.

However, what makes Bengal important in architectural history are the brick and terracotta temples which were built in the period after the dominance of Islamic architecture in India. The 17th to 19th centuries witnessed the emergence of a distinct Bengal school in an interesting series of temples in brick, which retained the indigenous architectural tradition, while incorporating certain features of Iranian or Sassanian techniques and forms, resulting in a unique group of temples combining the elements of different cultural traditions.

The multi-towered variety of the *nagara sikhara* here takes the form of the *panchayatana*. The structural *sikharas* are transformed into decorative ones, becoming a single massive construction, a huge tapering pyramidal tower on a square base surmounted by smaller towers rising on the four corners of the building. This mountain-like mass expresses the Meru conception of the north Indian medieval temple. It represents a curious blend of the Sassanian style of five domes and five cupolas and barrel vaults over a square, showing either a direct adoption of the Islamic vaulting technique, or a re-adaptation of forms that had earlier originated in

India and had been transferred to its west Asian neighbours. The Iranian and Islamic five-domed plan combined with the Indian five-tower elevation occurs in central Asia and in the five-domed Byzantine church, a style developed in the Roman empire of Contantinople during the 4th century.

The ground plan of the Bengal temple has been interpreted as a monumentalisation of the bamboo hut. The ground floor imitates the hut of a Bengal village, while the superstructure copies the tent of nomadic ancestors. In Bansberia (Anantavasudeva temple), the cubical structure with convex eaves is topped by an octagonal tower. The eight faces of the tower are pierced by ogive windows with horse-shoe-shaped cusped arches, which are probably derived from early Indian wood and rock architecture. Similar temples are found in Guptipara, Bankura and Sukharia, north of Calcutta. Sukharia has one of the largest groups of temples and a large tank for ritual ablution. It is in Bengal that the forms of the bamboo house of man, the temple car or the chariot of the god, and the brick temple, are alike in every detail, as in Guptipara. What distinguishes the temple from the dwelling house is the dark interior of the *garbha griha*, which retains its cave-like holy character and houses the stone or bronze image of the deity. Its exterior walls are decorated with terracotta panels depicting Hindu legends, particularly the *Ramayana* and the *Mahabharata* stories, as in the Anatavasudeva temple at Bansberia.

The influence of the Bengal house and temple type may be recognised even in Muslim architecture – in the 17th century Gaur tomb of Fath Khan on the border between West Bengal and Bangladesh. The shape of a Bengal house-like temple may be seen even as far as the Deccan, in the tombs of the 16th–17th centuries in Gulbarga and Golkonda, in Tipu Sultan's wooden palace in Seringapatam, and even in Mughal palaces, and in Humayun's tomb in Delhi and the Rajgir Jain temple on Vaidarbha Hill in Dhaka.

Above: *Interior corridor of the Jorbangla brick temple, Vishnupur, Bengal. The details of carving create a rich texture on the walls and decorative pillars.*
Below: *Terracotta panels of epic narratives, Vishnupur. These are commonly used in Bengal temples.*

■ *Gwalior and Mathura:* Islamic influences in Hindu architecture and vice versa are seen in a certain class of temples built after the establishment of Muslim rule in medieval India. In Gwalior, the Sas Bahu temple, with its cell now in ruins, has a hall (*maha mandapa*) in three storeys, in the form of open galleries or loggias surrounding the building on all sides, the effect of the facades being that of large open arcades, with their projections in a bold combination of contrasting planes. The ingenious interior arrangement has a central hall like a cross, where the nave and transcepts meet, a type which influenced some of the Islamic structures at Ahmedabad and Champaner in Gujarat.

Brindavan (Mathura), the most important centre of the Krishna cult during the period of the widespread Chaitanya movement, built at the end of the 16th century a group of five temples. Of these the Gobind Devi is the largest with a *maha mandapa*, a spacious cruciform structure (54 x 32 metres), similar to the Sas Bahu. They follow the *nagara* style, but mark an important change that had taken place owing to the Islamic domination in building art. Of great architectural beauty, these temples consist of a combination of balconies and loggias, of bracketed archways and moulded buttresses, wide eaves and ornamental parapets. Yet, with no figural carving, they lack spiritual content. The Brindavan temples rise from an octagonal plan and taper into a tall conical tower, with broad bands of mouldings outlining each angle, the surface effect being that of a series of diminishing rectangular panels.

■ *Kashmir:* The early phase of architecture in Kashmir was mainly Buddhist. The medieval Brahmanical movement led to a grand classical style in the 8th–9th centuries. Kashmir exhibits a remarkable difference, with no affinity to the main *nagara* style of north India. Here, the Graeco-Roman traditions of the early Christian era, as developed by the Buddhists, continued, with pillared porticoes and peristylar arcades. The method of construction shows practical proficiency in the bonding, cement and use of dowels. The Brahmanical temples are in ruins, but not to the extent of the Buddhist remains. The temple in the valley has only a central shrine and no assembly hall. The shrine was surrounded by a cellular peristyle, with a large gateway in the front like the *stupa* courts of the Buddhist monasteries of Gandhara (ancient north-west India). The prominent structural features are the pyramidal roof and a variety of fluted pillars, with a capital and entablature said to be of the Doric order. The roof composed of overlapping planks of wood, is derived from a wooden structure most suitable to the climate with its heavy winter snow.

The significant developments are of the 8th–9th centuries, as seen in the Sankaracharya temple on the Takht-i-Sulaiman, on a hill overlooking the city of Srinagar. The sun temple at Martand, which became the model for all subsequent Brahmanical temples in Kashmir, lies five miles from the ancient town of Anantanag. Though ruined, it shows all the above features, except for one difference – a detached portico in front of the central building, with two chambers in each of its wings. The temple stands on a high plinth (67 x 43 metres). The Martand sun temple and the Avantisvami Vishnu temple in Avantipur became the touchstones of the Kashmir style, which declined by the 10th century, although small shrines continued to be built even in the 12th century in more remote areas like Bilot.

In north India, temple-building activities virtually ceased in the medieval period with the establishment of

The Avantisvami temple, Avantipur, Kashmir, mid-9th century. The pillared corridor or peristylar enclosure around the temple is more like the peristylar cells of the early historic Buddhist monuments of Gandhara (Peshawar and Taxila region).

Muslim rule in the 13th century. However, major temple centres preserved the tradition and passed it on to the 16th–17th century artisans, who imbibed influences from the Islamic tradition and incorporated them into their architectural endeavours.

The Dravida Style of South India

Temple architecture in south India has an incredibly long history and continuity of traditions. Beginning from the 7th century, there was almost incessant architectural activity till the 17th century under various ruling families. Geographically, the temples of the *dravida* style occur in Tamil Nadu, Kerala, parts of Andhra Pradesh and Karnataka.

The period from the 7th to 9th centuries marks the first phase of its development, when the Pallava royal dynasty of Kanchipuram and the Pandyas of Madurai introduced the temple as a major institutional force to legitimise their sovereignty, and integrate the Brahmanical socio-political order. The Pallavas claimed with pride that they created temples without the use of brick, mortar and timber in their rock-cut cave temples and monoliths. They also used stone in structural architecture, thereby paving the way for the progression of the *dravida* style. Their temples are distributed all over the northern districts of Tamil Nadu, but the most significant are the rock-cut and structural temples in Mamallapuram

(Mahabalipuram) and Kanchipuram, their port town and capital respectively. The *dravida* style is characterised by a square shrine with a storeyed, pyramidal roof, each storey being marked by a string course of miniature shrines of various shapes, the square, apsidal and oblong. Pillared *mandapas* came to be added to this central shrine in an east-west alignment. The cave temple, which carries these basic features, consists of a cell or multiple cells at the back, with a pillared hall in front, which is sometimes carried on to the sides of the cell, as though the cell is surrounded by a pillared hall. In Mamallapuram, the cave temples show a great variety in the pillar design, the lion being a predominant motif (as the base, and rearing up on the pillar), as the Pallava emblem, both in the cave and structural temples. Narrative sculptures representing Puranic legends decorate the caves and are significant as political allegory and metaphors for power.

The monoliths, popularly known as the Panchapandava *rathas*, are in a class by themselves, a study in temple plans and designs, as each represents a form different from the other. Together they represent models of all the forms, used in the temple complex – the hut-like or tabernacle-like shrine, the square shrine, the oblong shrine and the apsidal one. The Pallava architects seem to have experimented with all these forms which were to become the basic design of the various components of the south Indian temple, particularly the shrine and the entrance *gopura*. Mamallapuram could well have been their main atelier. Some of the unfinished caves and monoliths show traces of the methods used by the artisans for cutting them from live rock.

The rock-cut style was evidently borrowed from the Buddhists, who developed it between the 3rd century BC and 3rd century AD in their huge *chaitya* and *vihara* caves in Bihar, in western India, and even carried down to the 8th–9th centuries in the Deccan at Ajanta and Ellora. However, it had limited potential for the Brahmanical religion, which served and flourished as an institutional force in an agrarian society in India from the 4th to 13th centuries. Temples had to be built in the plains and other eco-zones where huge rocky hills did not exist, and hence, the preference for the structural mode which had greater potential for an expanding agrarian order. Stones quarried from hilly areas could be transported over long distances to places where they were not available. Thus, there is a proliferation of structural temples in this region from the 7th to 13th centuries, and even upto the 18th century.

The *dravida* style progressed under the Pallavas who promoted the Puranic religion. The position of the images in various niches on the walls and their orientation was standardised by the *Agamas*, as norms for all temples, irrespective of their location and size. These texts were composed in different regions and reflect regional differences and forms of worship. The accent was on the verticality of the *vimana* (the main shrine) with its superstructure. Thus, we have the famous shore temple with two shrines for Siva, each with its storeyed spire, presenting a picturesque sight on the sea shore, with a courtyard now in ruins. Curiously, an oblong shrine for Vishnu in the reclining form, carved out of a single rock, is sandwiched between the two Siva shrines, marking the royal predilections for Saivism in the period of Rajasimha (AD 690–710), the most prolific temple builder of the Pallava dynasty. His magnum opus, however, is the Kailasanatha temple (Rajasimhesvara) in Kanchipuram, a jewel among Pallava temples, which has a *sandhara prasada* (double-walled shrine), with lateral and corner shrines attached to the main shrine. The shrine and the *mandapa* are together surrounded by a courtyard, with a running

series of sub-shrines, each with a small tower, rich in iconography, planned and designed as the *vastumandala*, symbolising the cosmos and standing as a metaphor for royal power. As the high point of Pallava temple architecture, it enshrines, like all other Pallava temples, the Somaskanda form of Siva in relief sculpture, combining Siva, Uma and Skanda, as the divine family to which the royal family is compared both in inscriptions and literary texts of the period. This sculpture is repeated in all the sub-shrines.

The Vaishnava counterpart of the Kailasanatha temple is the Vaikuntha Perumal temple, with three vertically arranged shrines for the three main forms of Vishnu (standing, sitting and reclining), yet another way in which cosmic symbolism is expressed. This temple has a unique series of historical sculpture narrating the story of a change in succession from one branch of the Pallavas to another, after tracing the mythical and historical origins of the Pallavas. Of great significance are the images in the niches of the temple walls which represent the *avataras* of Vishnu marking the change from the Vedic to the Puranic tradition. Other structural temples in Kanchipuram and in several other sites carry the *dravida* style forward, but the basic plan and design as established by the Kailasanatha temple are adhered to. This design continues with an accent on the verticality of the *vimana* in Tiruvadigai in south Arcot district, the direction in which the subsequent development of the style moved till it reached its meridien in the Chola temples of the 11th century.

The Pandyas excavated cave temples and monoliths on the hills surrounding Madurai, their capital city, and in the Tirunelvali district. Stylistically they are hardly different from the Pallava caves and iconographically too they carry the same narrative themes of the Puranic texts.

The Kailasanatha temple at Kanchipuram, 7th century AD. The vimana (shrine with tower) with its corner and lateral shrines attached to the double-walled main shrine with a storeyed superstructure of dravida style. The magnum opus of the great temple builder Rajasimha Pallava, the temple follows the Vastupurushamandala *in its cosmic symbolism, plan and design. See plan on p. 12.*

Following pages 50-51: *The huge pillared hall of the Ekamresvara temple, Kanchipuram. The temple elephant used during festivals in processions, is one of the grand royal symbols among the regalia of the lord of the temple, the divine sovereign with whom the temporal ruler compared himself through various metaphors.*

49

The *dravida* style reached the culmination of its development under the imperial Cholas, who, in their early phase, erected temples of modest proportions in various centres, each consisting of a shrine, an *antarala* and a *mandapa* with an enclosure and an entrance *gopura*. Signs of maturity in technology and aesthetic sense already mark these temples, but more importantly, a certain standardisation in iconography appears, indicating the formalisation of a canonical Agamic tradition. From narrative to icon, the movement is complete, and temples are repositories of the pantheon and the variety of forms assumed by the main deities.

The grand architectural enterprise, illustrated by the temples at Tanjavur and Gangaikondacholapuram in Tiruchirapalli district, is marked by bold innovation and patient rigour. These two royal temples of the 11th century represent the zenith of the *dravida* style, in architectural planning, design and the technology of building. Built of migmatite granite, the accent is on the verticality of the *vimana*, reaching new heights in Tanjavur (58.5 metres) and Ganagaikondacholapuram (50 metres). Tanjavur has a pyramidal roof with rows of miniature shrines attached to the stem of the *vimana*, but unlike the northern and central Indian *sikharas*, they are not separate but more like motifs of decoration. Less than the Tanjavur *vimana* in height, the Gangai tower is convex in outline and more rounded than the severe straight-edged pyramid of Tanjavur. South Indian temples are relatively more austere and severe in their design and decoration. In their straight-edged pyramidal form of the tower, they exhibit a balance in construction with a structural strength acquired by the method of balancing the weight and height of the superstructure in relation to the size of the temple.

The two royal temples have *vimanas* of the *sandhara prasada* variety with double walls and inner ambulatories connected by an *antarala* to the *ardha mandapa* with entries on the north and south guarded by the powerful figures of the doorkeepers (*dvarpalas*). The pillared hall in front is meant for ritual purposes and is approached by a *mukha mandapa* with flights of steps. All these components are in an axial line and in Tanjavur the whole structure is surrounded by a running veranda, with the shrines of the *dikpalas* and *lokapalas* located at the cardinal and intermediate directions. The whole enclosure measures, at its exterior, 234 x 117 metres (a 1:2 proportion). A moat and a rampart-like wall were added to it in the 17th century. With its two gateways aligned with the eastern approach, the

Brihadisvara temple in Tanjavur is a precursor and most probably a model for the grand temples of south India. These two gateways are forerunners of the future enclosures, with *gopuras* in ascending order of their heights, as seen in the horizontal expansion of the temples when the vertical accent was subsequently transferred to the outer gateways. Thus the sanctuary tower remained the dominant element, both in Tanjavur and Gangai, as also in the later Chola temples of Darasuram and Tribhuvanam in Tanjavur. Between 850 and 1279, some 300 temples, and between 985 and 1044, some 80 temples were constructed. Of these Tanjavur and Gangai alone represent a good one-fifth of all known Chola architectural activity.

Further development in the *dravida* style was in the horizontal expansion of the temple precincts, with an accent on the *gopura* tower and an increase in the enclosures, from one to three in the 12th–13th centuries, and from three to five or

The Siva temple at Darasuram, Chola, 12th century AD. More ornate than the severe symmetry of the earlier Chola temples, its decorative features are derived from the Chalukya style of the Deccan. The front mandapa *fashioned like a chariot on wheels drawn by horses is the chariot of Siva as Tripurantaka, a great warrior, who destroyed the forts of three demons, who subsequently became his devotees.*

Facing page: *The gopura or entrance gateway in one of the courts* (prakaras) *of the Minakshi temple, Madurai, a Nayaka period structure. The sikhara or tower with its several tiers of shrine motifs, brick and stucco images, plastered and painted, provides a tapestried effect.*

seven under the Pandyas, the Vijayanagara and post-Vijayanagara Nayaka rulers from the 14th to 17th centuries. The horizontal magnification may be attributed to several factors, such as the additions made by new royal patrons for legitimacy and continuation of a tradition; greater participation of the Saiva and Vaishnava communities; and the influential economic groups who contributed to the construction of subsidiary structures; shrines of *parivara devatas;* pillared halls for rituals, music, dance, dramatic performances and for gifts of daily offerings and festivals. Temples also had educational institutions attached to them, even from the 11th century, and hospitals with facilities for treatment and medicine, all of which were sponsored and patronised first by royalty and later by leading agricultural communities, merchant organisations and newly emerging socio-economic groups seeking to enhance their ritual status through the temple as the means of societal integration.

■ ***The Vijayanagara Style:*** The post-Chola architecture of south India is mainly that of the Vijayanagara period (14th–17th centuries), carried further by the Nayaka chiefs, who were the erstwhile subordinates of the Vijayanagara rulers. The initial and crucial stage of this development occurred in Hampi (Vijayanagara or

Vidyanagara in Karnataka), the capital of the imperial Vijayanagara rulers, founded in 1335. Here in the valley of the river Tungabhadra, Vijayanagara was established as the imperial city with a royal centre and a sacred centre, which developed side by side as multi-temple complexes. As an imperial city, which was to control the four different cultural regions of south India – Karnataka, Andhra Pradesh, Tamil Nadu, and to a lesser extent Kerala – the city had centuries of experience in architectural and art traditions to draw from, and Vijayanagara chose to carry further mainly the *dravida* style, and in some ways the Deccan traditions, in its art and architecture.

Architecturally, the temples of Hampi are impressive for their large and massive character. The chief temple in the sacred complex on the south bank of the Tungabhadra is dedicated to Virupaksha. Pampa, a local deity, became the consort of Siva as Virupaksha, the tutelary deity of the Vijayanagara kings. Of modest size, its sanctuary has features of the Deccan style elaborated with an enclosure and entrance *gopura*. The Ramachandra temple (early 15th century), the royal chapel in the middle of the royal centre, is the first major construction in the typical southern style with elaborate base mouldings, a pyramidal brick and plaster superstructure in its tower; and single pilasters emerging out of ribbed pots. Images, *Ramayana* reliefs and ceremonial courtly scenes on the enclosure walls also mark the southern influence.

The characteristic Vijayanagara style emerges only in the 16th century, its ambitious phase under its greatest rulers, Krishnadeva Raya and Achyuta Raya, when temples of the southern style of monumental proportions were constructed,

The Brihadisvara temple, Tanjavur, Chola,
11th century AD marks the culmination of
the dravida *style, in the vertical ascent of*
the vimana *(main shrine with tower),*
technologically superior to the earlier temples,
a stupendous royal project with the tallest
vimana *over 61 metres in height. It has 13*
tiers over a sandhara prasada *(double-walled*
structure), with an inner ambulatory at the
ground level enriched by narrative frescoes and
a second ambulatory on the first floor with
images of Siva performing the karana *or*
dance movements of the Natya Sastra. An
ardha mandapa, maha mandapa *and a*
small mukha mandapa *are in alignment*
with the shrine, located in a huge court with
an entrance gopura.

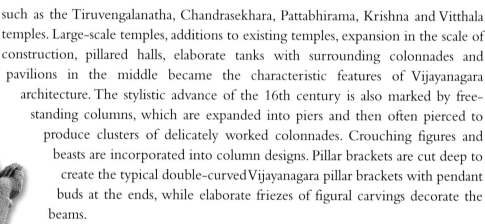

such as the Tiruvengalanatha, Chandrasekhara, Pattabhirama, Krishna and Vitthala temples. Large-scale temples, additions to existing temples, expansion in the scale of construction, pillared halls, elaborate tanks with surrounding colonnades and pavilions in the middle became the characteristic features of Vijayanagara architecture. The stylistic advance of the 16th century is also marked by free-standing columns, which are expanded into piers and then often pierced to produce clusters of delicately worked colonnades. Crouching figures and beasts are incorporated into column designs. Pillar brackets are cut deep to create the typical double-curved Vijayanagara pillar brackets with pendant buds at the ends, while elaborate friezes of figural carvings decorate the beams.

The huge gateway tower tapering upwards in a massive pyramid is one of the characteristic features of Vijayanagara architecture, identified with imperial magnificence and royal ambitions. Marked by ascending and diminishing storeys, the walls of the tower have niches for sculptural compositions, miniature roof forms on the tiers, rectangular vaulted roofs at the top, the whole being ornamented with deeply moulded plaster sculpture – in which vegetal, animal and other devices are freely mixed. There is an interesting complexity in the use of mouldings and projecting sculptured niches. Two types of *gopuras* were built, one, the straight-edged pyramid and the other, the tower with concave outline and rich stucco sculpture providing a tapestried effect. In Madurai, where there are 12 *gopuras*, both types are represented.

The horizontal magnification is best illustrated in the temples of Tamil Nadu, where the pre-existing temples of the sacred and political centres were consciously expanded by adding enclosures with 100 and 1000 pillared halls, sometimes separate and sometimes creating a maze of criss-cross halls and corridors, a feature which is pronounced under the Nayakas. Thus we have the famous Ramesvaram temple on

the south-eastern coast of the Tamil Nadu temple corridor, the 1000 pillared halls in Kanchipuram (the Varadarasvami temple with three enclosures), Tiruvannamalai (five enclosures), huge gateway towers at Chidambaram (four enclosures), and other innumerable sites where the Vijayanagara rulers announced their war glories in halls, gateways and inscriptions. Crouching and rearing animals, particularly horses and warrior figures, are prominent motifs on pillars, while figures of kings and chiefs as worshippers were added to the composite pillars of the Vijayanagara and post-Vijayanagara temples. The examples are numerous, and the Raya *gopuram*, as the entrance tower came to be known, dominates the temple landscape of south India today. Vijayanagara is also often associated with imperial and military architecture due to the vigorous and dynamic figural sculptures and massive architectural components in the temples. In Hampi, this is evident in the two complexes, the royal complex which includes, for the first time, secular architecture in the form of elephant and horse stables; the royal bath (Lotus Mahal), apart from the huge audience halls, of which only the stone basements now survive, while the wooden superstructures have disappeared. Yet they have decorative sculpture and base mouldings which are similar to those of the temples. The influence of Islamic architecture is also visible in these royal structures at Hampi.

■ *Kerala, A Different Experience:* Temple architecture in Kerala developed, like the rest of south India, during the early medieval period. Ideologically, the region has had closer links with Tamil Nadu than other regions of peninsular India, although its geography and ecology have been major determinants in its socio-cultural evolution. Hence the *dravida* style, which was adopted by royal patrons and the priestly elite, evolved certain distinctive features, especially to suit Kerala's climate and topography. The square shrine was replaced by the circular one, except in a few temples. Circular shrines could well have been influenced by earlier

Above: Vitthala temple, Hampi, 16th century, the most significant of the Vijayanagara temples at Hampi. The stone chariot seen at one end is in imitation of the wooden processional chariot of the deity.
Below: Simha mukha *(lion face),* a decorative motif popular in the Vijayanagara period.
Left: The Sesharaya mandapa *in the Ranganatha temple at Srirangam. The pillars of the hall have rearing horses with riders. Vijayanagara architecture reflects the imperial and military character of the Vijayanagara rulers.*

Above: Siva temple at Vadakkunnatha, Trissur, Kerala. It has a square shrine and circular mandapa, *both called* ambalams, *with overhanging eaves for easy drainage and protection from heavy monsoon rains. One of the largest temples in Kerala and an interesting example of a temple town.*
Below: *The rear wall of the shrine, Vadakkunnatha temple.*

Buddhist models, but also by the heavy monsoon rainfall. They help in the quick draining of the rains that normally lash this coastal land through half the year from May and intermittently in the other months. A similar purpose was served by the distinctive cornice, the long overhanging eaves, built of wood and tiles, which covered the circular and occasionally tiered pyramidal roof in stone, brick and mortar. The temple as a whole is known as *ambalam*, while the shrine and the *mandapa* are also individually referred to as *ambalam* and are similarly structured. The rectangular enclosure and the gateway complete the rest of the temple design. Yet, Kerala did not evolve any major architectural features which took the *dravida* style forward in the manner in which it developed in the Tamil region. The largest and most significant of the Kerala temples is that of Padmanabhasvami in Tiruvananthapuram, which in the 17th century, became the capital of Travancore under Marttandavarma, who ruled it as the temporal sovereign and representative of God Padmanabha, the divine sovereign of Kerala. This situation

is comparable to that of Orissa, which was ruled by Jagannatha, the divine sovereign, whose temple was erected at Puri by the Eastern Gangas, and later acknowledged by the Gajapatis of Orissa.

The Kerala temple roof, constructed on the laminated or clinker-built system of overlapping planks, is comparable to the tiered structures found in Nepal and some Himalayan hill-states and Kashmir. This kind of roof is reproduced in the temple cars or *rathas* of Orissa and other parts of the country, including the wooden chariots of south India, which are still fashioned of timber in this manner; each horizontal section takes the form of a wooden frame, with blocks fitted between, to keep each layer apart. It is also simulated in stone in the temple roof. In Kerala, the Mahadeva temple at Beypore, south of Calicut, and the Tiruvalla temple in Travancore appear to be of the double-roofed Nepalese variety. The 12th century Jain temples at Mudabidri, north-east of Mangalore, are of stone masonry, but copies of the wooden construction,

Above: *Mural on the walls with niches, the Trissur temple.*
Pages 58-59 (centre spread): *Siva temple at Perumanam, Kerala. The plan of the shrine is circular, rare in Indian temple architecture and followed only in regions of heavy monsoon and heavy glaciation as in Kerala, the Himalayan region and Assam or north-eastern India.*

common in the mountains of the north, and to a lesser degree, the stone temples of Kashmir. Such temples represent a common endeavour to solve the problems presented by the extreme changes of climate, in mitigating the effect of the fierce tropical sun, alternating with heavy monsoons rains or heavy glaciation.

■ ***Andhra Pradesh:*** This region also falls mainly within the architectural zone of the *dravida* style under Chola influence, particularly the river valleys of the Godavari and Krishna. However, its various sub-regions show the intrusion of architectural traditions from other cultural regions on its borders. For example, the north-western region of Andhra has temples of the Chalukya style of the Deccan, dating from the 7th–8th centuries, as those at Alampur. The Kakatiya temples of Telengana also followed the later Chalukya style of the Deccan, with some variations. Kakatiya architecture is a sudden outgrowth of the medieval situation with an upsurge of exuberant carvings and massive lathe-turned pillar forms. Warangal, Hanumakonda

and Ramappa have such monumental edifices. The northernmost coastal plains show the intrusion of the Kalinga (*nagara*) style in its early phases, while the rest of coastal Andhra has a predominant number of *dravida* style temples, particularly of the 11th and 12th centuries. The post 13th-century architecture of this region shows an extension of the Vijayanagara style, again predominantly a southern tradition, with its characteristic enclosures, pillared halls and gateways of monumental proportions. No powerful regional state emerged in Andhra Pradesh comparable to the Chola state of Tamil Nadu, which could encompass all the Telugu-speaking areas of Andhra Pradesh.

■ *Deccan, A Hybrid Style:* It is in the Deccan, known as Dakshinapatha in early texts, and now represented by Maharashtra and Karnataka, that the most remarkable and fascinating traditions of rock-cut and structural architecture came to be

AIHOLE, MEGUTI TEMPLE

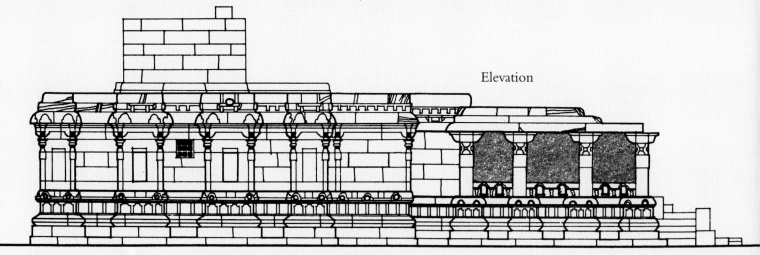

Elevation

Plans and elevations of the Aihole and Pattadakal temples exhibiting the development of a hybrid style mixing nagara and dravida architectural features. The dravida style is predominant in Pattadakal (see elevation). Puranic Hinduism influenced even Jainism, which adopted the temple as its institution of socio-religious integration as seen in the Meguti temple at Aihole under the Chalukyas of Vatapi (Badami). The Pattadakal temples are full-fledged Puranic temples of the Deccan style, remarkable as repositories of Puranic myths in their sculpture.

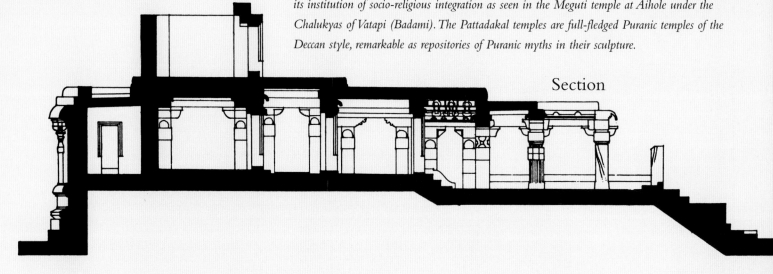

Section

→ N

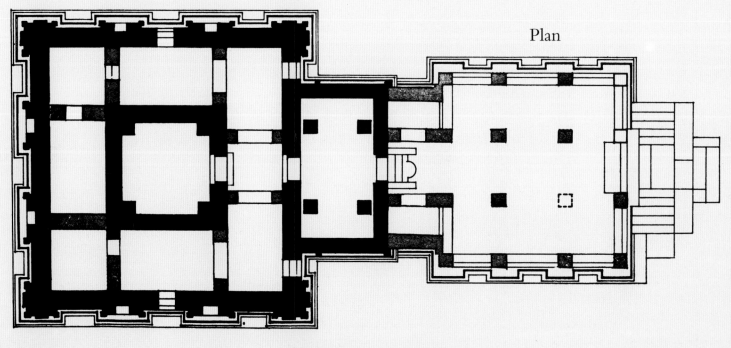

Plan

0   5M

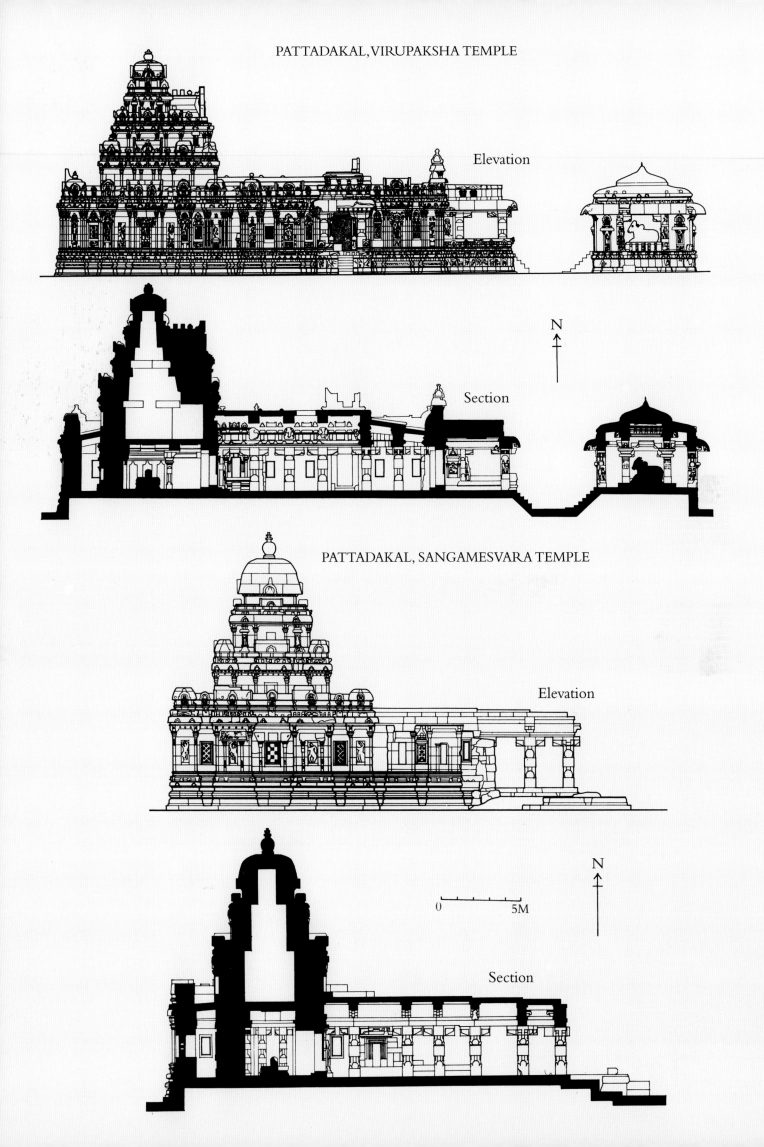

PATTADAKAL, VIRUPAKSHA TEMPLE

Elevation

N

Section

PATTADAKAL, SANGAMESVARA TEMPLE

Elevation

N

0   5M

Section

Pages 64–65 (centre spread): Durga temple, Aihole, 7th century. As no image survives in the sanctum, the temple may be of any Puranic deity and could be of either Aditya (Surya) or Vishnu. Architecturally the unusual apsidal shape of the veranda surrounding the shrine and its mandapa, suggests a Buddhist influence, for it is characteristic of the Buddhist chaitya or shrine. The temple is rich in sculpture of the Puranic deities.

Below: Siva as Kalasamharamurti, Pattadakal. According to a Puranic legend Siva saved the young devotee Markandeya, who was destined to live for only 16 years, by killing Kala or Yama, the god of death and changing the youth's destiny. Hence Siva is Kalasamharamurti.

developed from the 5th to 13th centuries. The rock-cut mode was first introduced by the Chalukyas of Badami, at two of the three major centres of their temple clusters at Badami and Aihole. Architectural activity at the three sites (the third being Pattadakal) created hundreds of temples, big and small, which appear to be great experiments in both the *nagara* and *dravida* styles. No single temple represented the diagnostic elements of either style in its entirety, but mixing or trying combinations and permutations resulted in such masterpieces as the Durga temple in Aihole, and the Papanatha and the Virupaksha at Pattadakal, among others. Aihole has a wide variety of temple plans; the pillared hall with a cell, located inside, resembling a congregational pavilion with sloping seatbacks (*kakshasana*), a feature which was to become a high point in the later pillared halls of the Deccan temples. The cell is gradually shifted to the back of the hall, thereby marking the position of the shrine in the temple design. Then followed a series of other experiments leading to the *nagara* style *sikhara* of the Durga temple, with a curious apsidal form in the veranda surrounding the shrine and its porch. The cave temples of Badami have remarkable panels of narrative sculpture representing the Puranic legends of Siva and Vishnu and

their iconic forms, powerful and dynamic in their composition and high relief, as if emerging out of natural rock. The structural temples at Badami and Mahakuta also show a similar experimental stage in the evolution of the typical Deccan style, a fusion of *nagara* and *dravida*.

Pattadakal, true to its name as the seat for the coronation of the Chalukyas, is unique in its group of temples, which carry the impress of the Deccan experiments in their final form, and with greater impact than the other two sites, due to the mature handling of the fusion of the two styles by the Chalukya artisans. The two most notable temples are the Papanatha and Virupaksha, the former adopting the *nagara* features, but using decorative motifs unknown in north Indian temples, the latter predominantly *dravida* in its design and execution, attributed by art historians to the southern influence of the Pallava temples of Kanchipuram.

The experiments of the Rashtrakuta ruling dynasty at Ellora (8th–10th centuries) are stupendous projects in cave architecture and monolithic temples. Although Buddhist and Jain caves continue to be excavated at the site in the form

Above: Siva as Ardhanarisvara, the hermaphrodite form combining the male and the female, i.e. Siva and Parvati, here shown with the Bull (Rishabha), the vahana *(vehicle) of Siva. Hence the image combines the Ardhanarisvara form with the Rishabhantika.*

of huge pillared halls with shrines at the rear, the Brahmanical ones are remarkable for their size and geometrically-arranged pillars, providing an amazing variety of views of sculptured panels. More important are the works of narrative sculpture in bold relief, unequalled by any other site, with Brahmanical narrative sculpture, such as Badami and Mamallapuram. The greatest achievement of the Rashtrakutas is the 8th century Kailasanatha monolith, cut out of huge rocky hills, in the *dravida* style, with a tiered-tower. It is more a sculpture gallery of great visual impact with numerous forms of Siva, Vishnu, and deities of the Saiva pantheon. Though large in

Below: A frieze of ganas or troops and attendants of Siva shown in different ways, as warriors in dancing poses. Ganas or yakshas *are dwarfish mythical creatures who make an amazing group of decorative motifs in friezes.*

Facing page: The plinth of a Hoysala temple which is common to all such temples of the 12th–13th centuries AD. The plinths have minute carvings with successive friezes of animals (elephant and horse) and floral and figural epic scenes from the *Ramayana and* Mahabharata. *Above these panels are wall spaces meant for icons and divine beings under floral canopies.*

size and designed imaginatively, its architectural and elevational impact is marred by the fact that it is located as if in a huge pit or hollow of a rocky hill, with the visitor looking down at the temple before climbing down to get a full and more impressive view.

Deccan, 11th–13th Centuries. A Fusion of Many Traditions: The later temples of the northern Deccan are conspicuously different from the earlier ones, as they derived their style from western and central India, and also from the rest of the Deccan. This kind of Deccan *sikhara* has a pronounced vertical band on each of its angles, taking the form of a spine, or from the cornice to the finial, holding the entire shape of the spire within its firm outline. The spaces within these are filled in with rows of small reproductions of the *sikhara* itself, each supported on a pedestal like an altar, the repeating pattern creating an unusual effect. In a similar fashion, the pyramidal roof of the *mandapa* is made up of diminishing rows of miniature multiples of itself in a singularly artistic design.

The plan of the larger temples appears as a diagonal arrangement. The elaboration in the shape of the walls, their projections and recesses create a curious interplay of light and shade as they mount upwards, giving an unusual vitality and variety to the elevation, as in the Jagadambadevi temple at Kokamthan. There is an amazing variety of pillar mouldings in the 11th–12th century temples at Ambarnatha in Thane district, near Mumbai in Maharashtra.

Later Chalukya and Hoysala Temples: The later Chalukya temples of the Deccan display a more integrated and aesthetic design. The plan is square and not stellate like the Hoysala temples. The interior ambulatory passage around the cell is lit by perforated stone windows. The principal entrances are not in front but often at the sides of the structure, as the eastern entrance is often faced by a supplementary cell, shrine or pillared portico. The pyramidal tower has an apex formed by a faceted, double-flexured bell shape. The niches on the walls are at appropriate intervals for images, with wide eaves running above the ornamental niches or shrines. The pillars are lathe-turned. The doorways at the entrance to the building and to the inner shrine show great artistry.

From the Kallesvara temple at Kukkanur near Gadag, to the Lakkundi Jain temples of the 12th century, the formation of the tower and its style matures at Chaudadampur (Dharwar district), with a wealth of plastic ornamentation and an innovative pattern in the *sikhara*, achieving its consummation in Lakkundi (Kasivisvesvara temple) and Kuruvatti (Mallikarjuna temple), all dating from the 12th century. The Gadag temples display a form of mural treatment which is carried forward in the temples of south Karnataka (Mysore). Like Belur and Halebid, each niche is shaped like a stele (niched figure sculpture), with a divinity carved in high relief. The stellate plan appears in the Dodda Basappa temple at Dambal, both in the

sanctuary and *navaranga*, a plan carried right up through the elevation of the building, the close array of vertical offsets creating a singular and arresting effect of chiaroscuro.

The Hoysala Style: The Chalukya-Hoysala builders (11th–13th centuries), unlike those of Dharwar, who made use of massive blocks of sandstone, resorted to a stone of much finer grain – a greenish or bluish-black chloritic schist. In the numerous temples built in the Mysore region, but for a few motifs of the northern style, the effect of the southern style is distinctly marked in the general plan and design, especially in the formation of the *sikhara*. The treatment of the wall surfaces, the design or order of the pillars, and the *navaranga* and open-pillared pavilion (*mukha mandapa*) are distinctive. Both single and multiple shrines are common, the latter with either a common *navaranga* or two or more *navarangas*. The plan of the outer wall of the sanctuary is laid out in a series of points, resulting in the figure of a star, or a stellate plan on the exterior. The stellate system is carried through the tower, even above the wide cornice, to produce a fluted effect on the tower above. An orderly succession of diminishing tiers, and a complex grouping of miniature shrines and niches decorate the tower with its low parasol-shaped finial. A high and wide platform runs parallel to the lines of the building, providing space for *pradakshina*. The plinth bands carry the well-known conventional sequence of processions of elephants signifying strength, horsemen denoting speed, spiral foliage and *kirtimukha* or sun face (a grotesque mask) and scenes from the epics. Then follow a border of *yalis*, a hybrid animal motif, a running pattern of *hamsas* (a legendary bird). Perforated stone screens and the *kakshasana* are other features of the pillared halls of this style.

The wall surface is decorated with ornate niches with foliated canopies under which are carved images of the gods, elaborately chiselled and appearing as a distinct and independent work of plastic art. The iconography is rich, as no important Puranic deity is left out from the pantheon of the religion to which the temple is dedicated. The pillars of the hall are monolithic and lathe-turned and enriched by a sloping bracket-stone fixed to them by sockets. These strut-like brackets are carved out of one slab into images known as *madanika* (female) figures, enshrined within leafy aureoles.

The Hoysala temples resemble sandalwood carving and ivory work. What the Hoysala craftsmen produced was in reality not architecture but applied art, which is similar to the intricate carving in western Indian temples of the medieval period. Typical examples are the triple-shrined Kesava temple at Somnathpur (65.5 x 54 metres), and the earlier and larger temples of Belur (54 x 47.5 metres). Belur has *madanika* figures even under the wide cornice outside. The Hoysalesvara at Halebid represents the highest achievement of this style. A double temple in every sense of the term, it has four entrances, two to each temple. It is visually rich, with a comprehensive sculpture gallery, a graphic record of the Hindu pantheon. The temple at Halebid has been described as the supreme climax of Indian architecture in its most superb manifestation and technical skill, ingenuity, imagination and profound religious significance.

Temple Towns

The growth of religious architecture in south India is inseparably linked with the growth of towns and cities, both developing simultaneously or in tandem. The temple formed the nucleus of organised ritual space, physical space and functional space for various social groups in a settlement, rural or urban. Such temple towns are numerous in Tamil Nadu, notable examples being Kanchipuram, Tiruvannamalai, Kumbhakonam, Srirangam and Madurai. They all have temples dating from the 7th or 10th centuries. However, later remodelling or renovation under the Vijayanagara and Nayaka rulers have either led to significant expansion of the temple precincts, while preserving the earlier shrines intact, or almost changed the temple's structure through ambitious remodelling (with additions of *mandapas*, enclosures and gateways of stupendous sizes), as in Madurai under Tirumalai Nayaka. Srirangam is the most perfect example, with seven concentric enclosures

Above: The sacred tank, Tiruvannamalai temple meant for ablutions and also for the float festival, when the decorated and ornamented deity is carried on a barge, worshipped with music and chants. It is invariably located in the outer enclosure of the huge temple complexes and serves different purposes, particularly at festivals.

Below: A decorated pillar with a rearing horse and rider at a temple in Srirangam.

Hoysala temple of Kesava, Somnathpur, 12th–13th century. A triple shrine with a common navaranga, the temple is surrounded by a courtyard and running peripheral veranda and entrance gateway. This is architecturally the most impressive of the Hoysala temples with all the characteristic features of the hybrid nagara and dravida architecture. It is unique in its stellar design on the outer projections, carvings from base to finial in a three-sectional elevation and a close affiliation to the west and central Indian schools in its sculptural treeatment, while the tiered construction of the tower is closer to the dravida vimana.

encompassing an area of more than 60 hectares, thereby incorporating most of the urban population.

Shrines of goddesses and other *parivara devatas* came to be added to temples from the 13th century onwards. The Vedic sacrificial pavilion built in the north-east corner of the courtyard became a regular feature in all temples from the 13th century when, in every Agamic temple, Vedic rites were introduced to consciously establish a Vedic association in all religious rituals and ceremonies. This hall is used at the time of the Brahmotsava or annual festival. With the increase in rituals and festivals, additions to the temple structure in the form of *mandapas* and courtyards (*prakaras*), with ascending gateways, led to the horizontal expansion of the temple. The *kalyana mandapa* (for marriage), *nritya mandapa* (for dance) and pavilions for religious discourses, for both ritual and entertainment purposes and for the innumerable functions of the temple, emerged. The community as a whole participated in these later elaborations. Ritual tanks called the *Brahma Tirtha* tanks often became a part of the temple in its outer enclosure.

The huge paraphernalia of ritual and administrative functions, which required space, also created a complex of structures like the kitchen, granary, treasury, *vahana mandapas* (halls for processional vehicles) and gardens within the temple precincts.

In large temple towns like Srirangam and Madurai, even the bazaars came to be located in the outer enclosures, while ritual specialists and executive functionaries of the temple and other elite of society had residential quarters allotted to them either within the enclosures or in the immediate vicinity. Instances of such towns are more numerous in south India. Historically significant developments in the institutional organisation of the temple took place in this region from the 9th to 17th centuries.

Temple towns are also known in north India, such as the sacred towns of Varanasi and Mathura, and the sacred-cum-political centres of Puri, Bhubaneswar and Khajuraho. Yet, the main difference between these and south Indian temple towns lies in the fact that these are morphologically not structured like south Indian towns, which encompass virtually entire towns within the temple complex, as in Srirangam and Tiruvannamalai, aligned according to the virtual plan of the temple, or with each temple as the focus of a settlement within larger multi-temple towns like Kanchipuram and Kumbhakonam. Conceptually, however, north Indian temple towns also have the temple as the focal point, but are often multi-temple centres with no clear alignment of the town's population, and with secular structures around the temple.

Varanasi (Banaras). A ghat on the sacred river Ganga which has several towns on its banks dating from the 6th century BC. Banaras is the most sacred of all, as it is a major pilgrimage centre for Hindus, Buddhists (Sarnath) and even the Jains. At the holy Saiva temple on the river bank, known as Kasi, people offer worship both to these deities and their ancestors, which bestows on them infinite religious merit. It is referred to as sacred in all religious literature, the Buddhist Jatakas and the Hindu and Jain Puranas.

Chapter 4

Idea and Image: The Iconography of the Hindu Temple

'INDIA THINKS IN IMAGES; THE IMAGE *(MURTI)* ITSELF IS BEHELD AS A DIVINITY.'

— Stella Kramrisch, *The Hindu Temple*

IT IS NOT THE INDIVIDUAL ICONOGRAPHY OF IMAGES, BUT THEIR configuration, or the iconographic programme as a whole that is important in a temple. The placement of the images, therefore, is highly significant. In fact, it was essential for the architect and sculptor to have knowledge of the pantheon and its ritual requirements, in order to correctly place the associate or *avarana* (surrounding) images in the temple. In this, they are guided by the *acharya*, who is well-versed in the religious system to which the temple belongs. Thus, the temple has the *achala*, or the permanent image, in the shrine and the other gods of the pantheon as well as subsidiary deities in the niches, and semi-divine, celestial beings in various parts of the structure. The *chala* or mobile images, made of bronze, are used for various ritual and ceremonial purposes, particularly processions, during festivals. Bronze-casting of images, on a large scale, from the early medieval times, heralded a period of ritual consolidation and artistic standardisation, and simultaneously of an imaginative variation of treatment of even well-known religious themes and legends.

The iconography of the Hindu temple evolved out of two basic concepts – *bhakti* or devotion to a personal god, and image worship – which are crucial to the development of the Puranic and Agamic traditions. Devotion to a personal god dominates the canonical texts, the *Puranas*. The *Puranas* created a huge pantheon for worship and perceived the temple as the house of god, where the chief deities were consecrated for worship. Around the main cult deities, such as Siva, Vishnu and Sakti, the Puranic mythology wove legends and stories of their greatness and divinity, establishing good and destroying evil, thereby giving rise to various forms of the deities, providing them with specific attributes and powers which determined their iconographic representation. The Puranic pantheon evolved out of a process of interaction between the Brahmanic/Sanskritic forms of worship, and a wide variety of local and tribal cults, beliefs and practices. It was a process of assimilation, which often meant that the local and popular forms were not merely absorbed but were given prime positions or predominance in the Brahmanical pantheon.

Thus, Siva acquired many forms as the destroyer of evil, personified as the demon *(asura)*, pitched against the gods *(devas)*. This symbolised *apasmara* (ignorance or

Preceding pages 76-77: Vijayanagara temple, Hampi, 16th century. With two large enclosures and a gateway, this temple is an example of the process of horizontal magnification of the south Indian temples, with the additions of structures for increasing rituals and festivals and the institutional role of the temple.

Facing page: A Nataraja image in bronze. Siva in the Nataraja pose performing the cosmic dance.

79

Adivaraha cave temple, Mamallapuram, 7th century AD. Vishnu in his Varaha incarnation, retrieving the earth (here the earth goddess) from the demon Hiranyaksha, who kept her hidden in the terrestrial region. The legend is significant as a metaphor for royal authority over the earth.

darkness) against knowledge or light. Shiva is also the lord of dance and music, the divine dancer (Nataraja) who performed the cosmic dance. The Saiva pantheon developed by absorbing and assimilating several folk and popular deities, cult practices and rituals, and beliefs. The aniconic *linga*, usually identified as a phallic symbol, was in many ways the most significant form, and it remains the cult object in all Siva temples (except the Pallava shrines), which helped in the assimilation of a wide variety of folk and fertility cults focussing on the pillar and the tree.

The concept of incarnation (*avatara*), specific to the other major deity, Vishnu, enabled the incorporation of folk and tribal deities and their cult practices into the Vaishnava religion. Thus, we have the Varaha or Boar incarnation, Narasimha or Man-lion and other human forms like Rama and Krishna among the *avataras* of Vishnu. The *avatara* concept is based on the famous Hindu holy book, the *Bhagavad Gita* (a text appended to the epic *Mahabharata)*. The text itself is revered till today as the divinely-ordained guide to *dharma* or norms of existence and conduct as preached by Krishna, who explains the concept of the *avatara* as the millenerian appearance of the divine, when world order disintegrates and divine interference brings back *dharma* by doing away with evil. This concept proved to be of immense value in creating several forms of Vishnu through a synthesis of the two traditions, The Great and The Little.

The *Puranas* narrate the legends and stories of the forms assumed by Siva and Vishnu, and the *Agamas* lay down their essential features and attributes, as guides to their representation in temple iconography. Regional variations in iconography appeared due to the degree and intensity of influence, and the assimilation of regional and local legends and cult forms into different pantheons. The technical treatises on temple building and icon-making (*Vastu* and *Silpa Sastras*) follow the *Agamas* closely, but at the same time lay down the actual methods of temple construction and iconic representations, as well as the material to be used. The principle of *talamana* or measurements adopted for the images in specific ratios, like the *nava* and *dasa tala*, following the human body (iconometry), plays a significant role. Thus, the religious and technological aspects are combined in the *dhyana slokas* or memorised verses to be uttered, while the images are produced by the *sthapati*, his associates and assistants. A tradition is thus passed on from teacher to pupil, generation after generation; and a community of artisans emerges in the process, with a special ritual status in the temple and the society that develops around it.

Each region gave birth to its school of artisans who generally followed the Agamic and Silpa Sastric formulae, improvising and improving at the same time within permissible limits, without deviating from the principles of iconography. It is in the decorative aspects and the manner in which the images were enshrined in niches that the innovative skill of the artist came to the fore.

Images and icons on the temple walls do not merely represent the different forms of the deities to whom the temples are dedicated, but also reflect religious syncretism, rivalry and synthesis. This is done in the form of images combining two deities (Harihara) or subordinating one to the other (Lingodbhava, in which Vishnu and Brahma are inferior to Siva). Other images show two deities fighting each other, one symbolically killing the other, or incorporating a rival deity in the pantheon of the dominant deity, and so on. The attributes given to the main deity, in the form of multiple heads or hands, with a variety of weapons, are derived from the legends associated with their origins, or stories of their victory over evil. Hence, they should not be wrongly understood as monstrous, or grotesque as many early Western art historians and writers did. The temple thus became the background for the visual display of all such legends and forms assumed by the chief deity, placed in prominent niches of the walls and other architectural elements, while the shrine housed the main deity in the form to which the temple was dedicated.

The temple then stands as the monumental record of the history of the Puranic religion, its interaction with other non-Brahmanical religions (Buddhism and Jainism), and its importance in society. The architecture of the temple is so designed as to accommodate a particular pantheon of power in its *garbha griha* and the *avarana koshtas*, either in a hierarchical order, or in the order of preference of the royal author of the temple. Thus, the temple and the image are inseparable elements of a single scheme or project, meant to convey different levels of meaning through the design, organisation and orientation of the structure and its decorative sculpture. The historical context and the ideological developments need to be understood in order to

Ganesa being worshipped. This is an impressive medieval Kalinga style sculpture from Orissa.

place the stages of the evolution of the concept and the image, which are closely interlinked in the process of the temple's evolution from a mere cult centre to an institution of monumental proportions. Royal temples illustrate this more forcefully than temples which were the focal points of settlements, rural and urban. The latter follow the *Agamas* for their iconographic programme – a standardised formula. For example, in the Saiva temples, the images of Dakshinamurti on the south, Lingodbhava on the west or the rear wall, Brahma on the north, are laid down as the standard, although additional niches may carry images of Durga, Vishnu and other forms of Siva, depending on the size and location of a temple. In the Vaishnava temples, the shrine has one of the three conventional forms of Vishnu (seated, standing or reclining), while the incarnations are found on the exterior walls, except in some cases where the main deity (in the shrine) is one of the *avataras*.

The royal temples, on the contrary, had a specific purpose – to convey a political message about royalty, power and authority. Particularly significant are the temples built by major dynasties like the Pallavas, Cholas (Tamil Nadu), Eastern Gangas (Orissa), Chandellas (Khajuraho, central India) and Vijayanagara (Hampi, south India) – all architecturally magnificent and iconographically rich and innovative as metaphors symbolising royal power and reflecting the court ambience, ideology and military glory of the respective ruling families. In such temples, while the standard

Agamic formulae are undoubtedly followed, the focus is more clearly on the glorification of royalty through themes and images chosen to establish the equation of royalty with divinity. The iconographic programme was thus meant to convey the identity of the spiritual and temporal authority. In pre-modern periods of history, the divide between the religious and sacred, and the secular and temporal, was unknown, and royalty was the visible symbol of divinity and temporal authority, inseparable from spiritual authority. Ancient and medieval kingdoms in India and, in fact, in many regions of Asia, created the temple as the superordinate institution for establishing this near-total identity, thus making it an ideological apparatus for the establishment of territorial authority. Icons enshrined in the temple and its niches created a political iconography with various levels of meaning behind the apparent religious function. A selective group of iconic themes are presented here to explain the allegory and metaphor in narrative and icon in the temple.

Iconic Forms of Siva

Allegory is used everywhere in the Pallava cave temples. Forms of Siva, which depict his exploits, are used as narratives of power in panels and individual icons. The descent of the Ganga is a major theme for a huge narrative in an open-air rock relief in Mamallapuram, and also on other panels where Siva carries Ganga on his head. Narratives serve multiple purposes, while popularising epic and Puranic legends. The Gangadhara form of Siva has a special significance in the Pallava cave temple at Tiruchirappalli, where the accompanying inscription claims that in the making of the image, the king 'himself became immortal together with Siva in the eyes of the world'. Unique and innovative as the cult object in Pallava temples, the Somaskanda form of Siva, a composite icon, was intended as a metaphorical portrait of the royal family. This is confirmed by the inscriptions and literary texts of the

period, as also the monumental Kailasanatha temple at Kanchipuram, which is a veritable storehouse of Puranic and Agamic religious themes. The Tripurantaka is a form of Siva, almost exclusively depicted in south India.

Siva, in both his benign and terrible aspects, provided a variety of metaphors. However, it is the *linga*, the aniconic phallic symbol, which is the most interesting for symbolic representations. One of the multiple ways in which the *linga* was used was the *mukhalinga* with four or five faces.

Rajasthan temples show a predominance of the *linga* and its varieties, both as a phallic emblem and as a *mukhalinga* with either four or five faces. The Mahesamurti, also a form of *mukhalinga*, has on its four sides, Brahma, Vishnu, Surya and Siva. In Elephanta island off Bombay, a powerful sculpture representing a different form of Mahesa, combining the terrifying and the female aspect, occupies a whole wall surface of the main cave and is legitimately famous for its scale and conception.

The Kalyanasundara form represents the marriage of Siva and Parvati, a favourite theme in south Indian sculpture and bronzes. Its importance is evident from the numerous bronze and stone icons in the temples, but even more for the celebration of the marriage as a major festival in all Siva temples. Madurai is the most important centre for the festival. In early north Indian works of sculpture, there are images of Himavan (the father) and Mena (the mother) giving away the bride, Parvati, to Siva. In later works of sculpture, they are replaced by Vishnu and Lakshmi; the relationship of Vishnu as Parvati's brother was introduced mainly in south Indian myths.

Siva as Mahayogi and Lakulisa (an ascetic of the extreme form of Saivism known as Pasupata, meaning the protector of animals) is common in Rajasthan, Khajuraho and Orissa. The Pasupata sect, of which Lakulisa is the central deity, had its origin in north India. Much later in the 12th century, the Chola temples of south India

Left: Siva as Ardhanarisvara with his vahana, the Bull, a syncretic form in which the female Sakti (goddess Parvati) is given the left side of the body of the hermaphrodite form.

Right: Chandesanugrahamurti, a form of Siva which had special associations with the devotional movement of the Nayanar, one of whom, Chandesa, was such a devout follower that he did not hesitate to cut off his father's leg which hit the Siva linga that he worshipped. Pleased with his devotion, Siva made him the guardian of his temples. This sculpture is the most elegant of the figures representating this form, as it is in the act of accepting the devotee by tying a garland on his head, a supreme honour for any worshipper.

Kartikeya (Subrahmanya) on his peacock. A warrior god and leader of the army of the gods, he is better known as the second son of Siva. As a folk deity of the Tamil kurinchi *region (hilly tracts), he is Murukan, a child god and retains his early popular associations, despite his incorporation into the Saiva pantheon and specially into the composite icon of Siva as Somaskanda in the form of the child Skanda.*

introduced this form, evidently as a result of the incorporation of all extreme sectarian beliefs and practices in the Saiva fold.

Nataraja, the dancing Siva, is perhaps the most important of Siva's forms, known for its beauty and variety. Its representations in south India remain unparalleled by any other region's art, although the dancing form is invariably included in the temple iconography of all regions, as he is considered to be the 'originator of all arts', particularly dance. The Nataraja figures and the execution of the dance movements (*karanas*) in north India are in many ways different from those of south India. North Indian sculptors preferred the tender modes of dance (*sukumara nritya*), as in Rajasthan and central India. The less benign and more malevolent forms are also known in these regions, where Siva is represented as dancing among the *matrikas* (divine mothers) while playing the *vina* (a predecessor of the *sitar*), the dance being witnessed by the gods.

The Ananda Tandava form of Siva is a remarkable canonical form of Nataraja performing the dance of bliss, which was codified under the Cholas. Siva danced on various occasions and at different places, including the graveyard. Nataraja's dance is of cosmic significance and has been associated with the five acts of creation or evolution (*srishti*), protection or preservation (*sthiti*), destruction (*samhara*), removal of illusion (*tirobhava*) and liberation or salvation (*anugraha*). His dance, on various occasions, is described as the dance of omnipotence or dance of victory (where he is Tripurantaka), of omniscience (with the *vina* or the lute), of time and eternity (Kalantaka). As Ardhanarisvara (the hermaphrodite form), his dance is of creation. He is also represented iconographically while dancing with Vishnu and Brahma. The dance of bliss, victory and creation are known to north Indian iconography, while the supreme Ananda Tandava form is a contribution of south India, as described in a 14th-century text called *Kunchitangristava* by Umapati Sivacharya, a great philosopher of the Saiva Siddhanta system.

Many other concepts are linked to the Nataraja aspect, and the Ashtamurti or eight-fold form became popular even in Cambodia. Nataraja, the most dynamic of Siva's forms had a special significance for the Cholas, who performed their coronation in Chidambaram, the major canonical temple of the Saivas which represents a happy blend of Siva and Vishnu in the Nataraja and Sayana forms, both of which are enshrined within the same temple complex.

Seven *tandavas* (dances) are mentioned in the Hindu texts on the arts and nine in the *Silpa Sastra* of the 16th century. The dance of Nataraja has its own cultic geography identified with seven centres, of which the Himalaya is one, while the rest are in south India; Madurai and Chidambaram are the important ones. The movements created by his dance are described in beautiful metaphors by Kalidasa, the great poet of classical Sanskrit (4th–5th century).

Siva was himself *natya* (dance) and *natyacharya* (teacher of dance). This imagery was created by both the Sanskrit and Tamil texts and the south Indian sculptors have rendered it in remarkable works of sculpture in stone, and more significantly, in bronze. Since Siva is the originator of all arts, especially music and dance, dance poses are often illustrated in various architectural components of the temple, such as the doorways of the *gopuras* (as at Chidambaram), pillared halls meant for dance performances, and so on. Live dance performances have recently returned to the Chidambaram temple in the form of a festival held every January.

Vishnu in Narrative Art and Iconography

The concept of the *avatara* associated with Vishnu from very early times led to the evolution of several incarnations of the deity, of which ten came to be standardised by the 7th–8th centuries. The epic origins of this concept were carried further by the Puranas by introducing various incarnations capable of assimilating and incorporating popular, folk/tribal forms into the purely mythical, theriomorphic and hybrid (human and animal) forms, as well as purely human forms assumed by Vishnu to re-establish *dharma* in periods of crisis. This change from Vedic to Puranic is best illustrated in the Pallava temples, the Vaikuntha Perumal temple at Kanchi marking this change. This temple has panels representing Vishnu as the deity who recovered the Vedas from oblivion and protected the gods from the demons. Directly influenced both by the Sanskrit texts (*Bhagavata Purana*) and the Tamil *bhakti* hymns of the Vaishnava saints, this artistic rendering of the Puranic pantheon appears on the sculptured panels on the *vimana*, which is itself conceived as a vertically arranged triple shrine signifying cosmography. The temple also significantly carries historical sculptures of the Pallava dynasty originating from Vishnu in the pillared corridor surrounding the *vimana*.

Among the incarnations or *avtaras* of Vishnu, the Varaha or huge boar is found in some north Indian temples. The Varaha in front of the Lakshmana temple at

The theriomorphic form of Varaha (Vishnu), Khajuraho, 12th century, symbolising in his body the cosmos, carrying all beings divine and human. Such representations of the boar form of Vishnu are known from the 5th century AD.

Khajuraho carries on its body all the heavenly bodies and other features symbolising its cosmic character. The concept of royalty or regal power is also associated with the boar in the religious and court literature of medieval India. It has been a political metaphor ever since the Gupta period, as seen in the famous Udayagiri cave sculpture of a huge Varaha in its hybrid form. The Pallava narrative sculptural works represent the *avataras* of Vishnu, like the Varaha and Vamna-Trivikrama, who retrieved the earth from the demons, as metaphors of royal control and protection of territory.

The reclining (*seshasayi*) form of Vishnu, yet another image of cosmic significance, is a purely southern icon, often enshrined in temples of great antiquity like Srirangam, Kanchi and Kumbhakonam, apart from Tiruvananthapuram. This form is rare in the north, as no shrine has it as the main deity, although, possibly under southern influence, several relief sculptures decorating the *vimana* walls were introduced in Rajasthan and central India.

Among the other *avataras,* Narasimha, the Man-lion, is represented both singly in an iconic form and also in combat with the demon, Hiranyaksipu, in the caves of the Deccan and structural temples of other regions. Rama is rare in temple sculpture till at least the 10th century, when this royal figure became the main deity in some south Indian temples, while scenes from the epic *Ramayana* were increasingly

depicted in sculptured panels in parts of north India and many regions of peninsular India. The Pratiharas, a Rajput dynasty, trace their descent from Lakshmana, the brother of Rama.

Krishna, the most beloved of the *avataras*, is known from sculpture more as part of the scenes from the epics and the *Bhagavad Gita*, than as an independent icon in India. Once again, it is in south India that temples were dedicated to this *avatara* as the Lord of Dvaraka, from the 10th century. *Krishna Lila*, the story of Krishna's life and powers, particularly of his childhood exploits and of his attraction to *gopis* (female cowherds) became the most favoured themes in the sculpture of north India, particularly Rajasthan. Equally popular was the *govardhana* episode in which Krishna protected the cowherds from the severe rains caused by Indra, the Vedic deity, who controlled the clouds and rains. Krishna bronzes of south India, dating from the 10th century, are predominantly those of Kaliya *mardana* (Krishna killing the serpent-demon Kaliya who tried to poison the Yamuna river) and of *Dvarkapati* or the king of Dvaraka with his consorts, Rukmini and Satyabhama.

Puranic Cults and their Pantheon of Deities

Puranic religion developed in India through centuries of interaction among popular, folk and tribal cults and forms of worship, and the mainstream Sanskritic forms of worship. The pattern of evolution differed from region to region and diverse cult deities were incorporated into the mainstream by a synchronic and sometimes diachronic process of acculturation into the two major Puranic systems, Saiva and Vaishnava, and that of the cult of the mother goddess or Sakti. However, popular and folk deities often retained their original traits, a phenomenon of great

Above: Kailasanatha temple, Kanchipuram, 7th century. Durga, a favourite icon in Pallava art, on her lion, eight-handed and holding several weapons.
Below: Mahishasuramardini cave, Mamallapuram. Durga fighting Mahisha, the buffalo-demon depicted in a large sculptured panel.

regional importance. Hence, Puranic structures were consciously adopted to preserve their cultic significance. It is this pluralism and regional diversity that sustained the continuous development of the Puranic religion, and in fact, made it a general paradigm for all sectarian canonical traditions. Thus we have the *panchayatana* or worship of five main cults for which temples came to be erected from the 6th century in the whole of the subcontinent. A sixth was added in the Tamil tradition, that of Murukan or Subrahmanya, an early Tamil deity whose identity came to be merged with the Sanskritic Kartikeya, the warrior god. The six major cults thus are those of Siva, Vishnu, Sakti, Surya, Ganesa and Subrahmanya. Siva and Vishnu are the two main Puranic gods, while the rest were assigned positions of power in a graded hierarchy in the two main pantheons. Siva and Vishnu and their iconography have been graphically presented earlier. The others are now presented.

■ *Sakti:* Sakti or the goddess cult is perhaps the most ancient and widely prevalent in India, each region having its own specific aspect of the goddess as central to her worship. Her incorporation into the Puranic religion took a variety of forms, as an independent deity, both benevolent and malevolent, as the consort of Vishnu and Siva, or as the mother goddess in the *sapta matrika* forms representing the female energies of the male deities, and so on.

Sakti worship was derived from the early female deities of folk/popular religion. The mainstream Brahmanical religious systems incorporated most of them as consorts of male deities, such as Parvati, Lakshmi, and so on. However, from very early times, the female Sakti or the Goddess as Power retained her individual status in many forms. One of them is the *mahishasuramardini* aspect of the female goddess, in which the buffalo-demon is defeated and killed by the deity. This is popular in the whole of India and the goddess is represented either in combat with the buffalo-demon or independently as Durga. Of the narratives of this Durga and demon conflict, the most remarkable are those from the Rashtrakuta caves at Ellora and the Pallava caves at Mamallapuram. The iconic forms are equally important in Siva temples, with a special niche assigned to the goddess on the north wall of the *vimana*, as per Agamic standardisation. Durga continues to be the most favoured among the female goddesses, and during festivals associated with her, the making of her images take many interesting and imaginative ways, as in Bengal, where the skills of the image-makers are highly visible.

The *sapta matrika* aspect (divine mothers) shows the female Saktis in a group following Siva, with Ganesa, on lintels, doorjambs, and as separate figures in north India and the Deccan. Other goddesses, like Lakshmi (accompanied by elephants) and Saraswati, are worshipped all over the country for wealth, prosperity and learning respectively, and hence, find a place in the iconographic scheme of the temple.

An unusual and less known cult, the worship of *chunshat yoginis* (64 *yoginis*), probably a Sanskritised form of the worship of tribal deities, developed in the central Indian tribal belt, where temples on a circular plan were built in the 10th–11th centuries, as at Khajuraho and Hirapur. The figures of these goddesses are depicted with a rare sense of beauty and elegance. They are not worshipped any longer, but have survived as statues of great merit and antique value.

■ *Surya, the Sun God:* Surya is the only Vedic god who came to be given a Puranic orientation. Due to his Vedic association, and foreign impact, his early images were of the standing Persian type. Images of the sun riding on his chariot drawn by seven horses were common. Initially worshipped as an independent deity with his own temples, Surya lost his separate identity by the medieval period, becoming a part of the main Saiva and Vaishnava pantheons, due to a syncretism between Surya and Vishnu (Surya Narayana in Rajasthan and Gujarat), and between Siva and Surya (Martanda Bhairava, also in Rajasthan, and parts of north India, and rarely in south India), and between Surya and the Trinity (Khajuraho). Yet he remained a part of the *panchayatana* cult and its worship.

Kailasa temple, Ellora. Images of sapta matrikas *(seven divine mothers) found in many of the Siva temples of north India and the Deccan. This temple is a veritable sculpture gallery of the 8th century Puranic deities. The Puranic tradition had its most glorious period of development in the early medieval period from the 6th to 12th centuries AD.*

■ *Ganesa:* Ganesa functions on multiple levels in the hierarchy of Indian gods. He is one of the subsidiary gods as well as one of the supreme deities, and his worship crosses sectarian boundaries. Ganesa's folk origins can be recognised in his hybrid form – elephant head and human body. He appears in Indian literature from the 5th century onwards. Myths about him were developed predominantly in the Puranas to explain this form, according to which Siva cut off his head in a violent physical confrontation with him, when as the guard of his mother, Parvati's inner chamber or bath (symbolic of her sexuality), Ganesa prevented Siva from entering it. The elephant head was placed on his body as a substitute, after reconciliation and

revival. Ganesa was then appointed as the leader of Siva's army of *ganas* (dwarfish mythical creatures known for their strength and valour), hence he is Ganapati or lord of *ganas*.

Ganesa is invoked for mental agility and learning, which is probably one of the reasons he is assigned the role, according to myth, as the scribe for Vyasa's dictation of the *Mahabharata* in the 8th-century interpolation to this text. His description as a child — devoted to his parents (particularly his mother), clever, comic and greedy — has been the basis of many stories illustrating his traits. He is the integrator of opposites and has both a negative and positive aspect in his dual role as creator and destroyer of obstacles. Ganesa's role as door guardian and as the lord of beginnings places him invariably at the point of transition. He is worshipped first when one enters a Siva temple.

The Puranic Ganesa is well-defined as the son of Siva and Parvati, yet in art and ritual his dual role is more important, and hence, Ganesa is presented as an icon to be propitiated. No myths and narratives about him are developed in art. Ganesa begins to appear in art from the 6th century as Siva's son, as seen at Elephanta. He is not found in the epics except as one of the *vinayakas* (demi-gods). He is associated with a variety of goddesses in ambiguous roles of both son and husband. There are important regional differences in the perceptions of Ganesa, and even each individual's perception varies dramatically. His adaptability in a variety of contexts is exemplified by the way in which he is worshipped before beginning any task, and as member of the Saiva pantheon and in Tantric rituals. He is associated with the divine mothers (*matrikas*) from the 4th–5th centuries, as seen in the works of sculpture at Udayagiri in central India.

Subrahmanya with six faces (Shanmukha). A legend about the birth of Kartikeya/Subrahmanya associates him with six divine maidens, blessed by Lord Siva. As all the six became the cause of his birth, he is given six faces. This form is more popular in south Indian iconography, where temples of Subrahmanya have different forms.
Facing page: *Ganesa, dancing. Bronze figure. The god of beginnings, who removes all obstacles, is worshipped at the start of all festivals and ceremonies and is represented in a variety of ways, including dancing. A popular theme even today.*

■ *Subrahmanya, the Kaumara Cult:* Puranic religion incorporated yet another popular deity into the Saiva pantheon — the second son of Siva called Skanda or Kartikeya and also Subrahmanya. This was the more popular Tamil deity called Murukan who came to be identified with Skanda. The Brahmanical acceptance of this local deity as predominant in the Saiva pantheon assisted in the development of Puranic religion in south India. The Murukan cult is the most significant of all regional cults, developing its own sacred geography and combining Vedic-Puranic elements with ancient and popular forms of worship. At times of crisis and challenge to mainstream Brahmanism, it was by elevating the subordinate deities in the pantheon to centrality in temple worship that a wider popular base was created for the Puranic religion. Subrahmanya's characterisation as a warrior god (Skanda – the lord of the divine army), a child god (Murukan), a handsome bachelor (Kartikeya), and the supreme giver of knowledge (Brahmanya) are part of the Puranic process of myth-making and acculturation. In the *panchayatana* worship in north India, he does not figure at all. As Skanda-Kartikeya, the mighty warrior, this deity has been an important part of the Hindu pantheon all over India from the beginning of the Christian era.

Chapter 5

Puja, Utsava and Tirtha: Ritual Worship, Festivals and Pilgrimage

✱

IT IS BELIEVED EVEN TODAY THAT STRUCTURAL ELEMENTS AND rituals merge and infuse an aura of divinity that pervades the temple, its activities and environs. Ritual worship or puja is an organised set of daily rituals in a temple. They start with waking up the deity with chants and music, followed by the first of the five or six main pujas of the day. Twice the deity is given a sacred bath (*abhisheka*) and decorated with beautiful garments and ornaments. This is done to the stone *linga* and to the bronze images in Siva temples, and to both the main and other images in the Vishnu temples. The offering of food (*naivedya* or *bhoga*) completes the morning *upachara* (literally hospitality, but in temple terminology, it is an offering or homage to the divine sovereign). After the dawn puja, various objects such as a mirror, parasol, fan, flag, emblem, fly-whisk, incense, lamps and camphor are offered to the sound of bells and temple music, accompanied or followed by chants of invocation, dedication and praise. Distribution of *vibhuti* (sacred ash) or *kumkuma* (holy red powder), as well as *prasada* (residue of the food offered to the deity) is then carried out. Then follows the noon puja, *sandhya* (twilight) puja and *ardha jama* (midnight) puja, and putting the deity to sleep ceremonially. These are part of the *shodasa maha upachara*, or the 16 kinds of great offerings to the deity, a ritual which was also, at one time, ceremonially performed for the king at his palace.

For the devotee who goes to the temple to worship, the *darsana* and *archana*, seeing and performing puja take place after the morning and evening *upacharas*, when the priest, as the mediator, performs the puja on the devotee's behalf. The devotee himself does the ritual of *pradakshina* or circumambulation, the significance of which lies in his visual and spiritual experiencing of the divine by passing round the surrounding niches, seeing the images or manifestations of the deity, and finally reaching the threshold to the shrine, the point of transition from the mundane to the spiritual. Here, he waits to be transported to the divine presence by the priest-mediator. Chants and music at every stage of the daily puja enhance the atmosphere of the temple's sanctity. Sandalwood paste, incense, flowers and the waving of lighted camphor and lamps in the inner shrine further emphasise the mystique of temple worship, of both the personal worship by the individual and the congregational worship by the devotees on festive occasions, each complementing the other. The atmosphere is charged with the scent of flowers, the burning oil lamps and the aroma of the incense from the sanctuary, intensified by the impact of the pillars and carvings of the congregational hall.

Religious rites are charged with different levels of meaning and significance. The clockwise circumambulation by the devotee is the most common. Worshippers make

Facing page: Kailasanatha temple, Kanchipuram. The deity in procession with his consort in regal attire, decorated and ornamented, during the Sivaratri festival. Florists weave various patterns of garlands and ritual specialists decorate the idols after a bath using unguents and perfumed water, milk and honey. The silken garments and jewels are made by weavers and goldsmiths specially appointed for the temple's requirements.
***Below:** Vishnu temple, Mylapore, Chennai. An idol of Vishnu, dressed and decorated with ornaments and flowers for the procession.*

an auspicious *pradakshina* of the central shrine and then the other subsidiary shrines. The myths associated with a particular temple are re-enacted when the *pradakshina* is performed around other sacred symbols of a temple. For example, the circumambulation of the mango tree in the rear court of the Ekamranatha temple at Kanchi is believed to be an act of homage to the earth *linga* under the tree worshipped by Parvati (according to legend) for union with Siva.

Ritual music, especially the singing of *bhakti* or devotional hymns, for which endowments are known to have been made from the 9th century, continue to this day, adding to the religiosity of the worshipper and the community consciousness of the devotees. Dancers and musicians have for centuries been involved in daily and periodic festivals, for which they have been remunerated with houses and land. In Tanjavur alone, the Chola king, Rajaraja I (11th century), employed 400 temple servants, including dancers and musicians. Temple dancers formed a very important part of the service personnel of the temple from very early times. They were servants of the god, but patronage came from the ruling families, the landed and other elite members of society.

The institution of the *devadasis* (women slaves of gods) is a legacy of this socio-religious organisation in medieval times, when female and male dancers were appointed. The female dancers, 'married' to the deity of the temple, became specialists in the ritual, and hence the service assumed a hereditary character, like all other services in the temple. Thus they began to cater to royalty, and other elite classes. This professional group later crystallised into a caste. This institution developed most conspicuously in regions in which the temple's ideological role in society is historically well-attested, as in Orissa, Karnataka and Tamil Nadu.

Above: The fly-whisk waved by priests during daily rituals and festivals to the accompaniment of music and chants.
Below: An incense holder, also waved in ceremonial ritual at the temple every day at the five or six pujas being performed among the 16 types of upacharas *or services.*

Festivals

Historically, festivals evolved around the myths and legends of the particular aspect of the deity enshrined in the temple, and the popular beliefs encoded into the temple's origin myths. They grew in number and importance depending upon the temple's locale, the founder-patron, and their significance for the community. Birth asterisms of the royal family and of Bhakti saints and spiritual leaders were important occasions for institutions. Festivals, particularly for religious leaders, continue to this day. Other festivals to celebrate the gods' victory over evil forces/demons, which have been basic to the Puranic religion, are still observed in all the temples. Festivals associated with Siva, Vishnu, Kali (Durga) and Subrahmanya are celebrated in their respective temples. Durga killing Mahishasura is amongst the major myths celebrated in these temples. Processions of the deities, regally attired and ornamented, on their decorated *vahanas* (vehicles), or in their chariots, are still major events in sacred centres on all such occasions. These processions have their counterparts in royal processions, about which poetic compositions are known from the 11th century. On such occasions, the interface between the sacred and the secular is highly visible.

■ *Brahmotsava:* Festivals in general display a cyclic concept of time. Brahmotsava, the only festival at which a flag is hoisted in temples, is conceived of as the close of a cycle (the end of a period of dissolution) and a fresh beginning. This is the grandest and most eventful of festivals, and the annual festival in each temple, believed to be celebrated by Brahma, and hence called Brahmotsava. The usual season for this festival in south India are the months of April–May (Chittrai), but it is also celebrated at other times as in the Varadrajasvami temple at Kanchi, where it begins after the harvest (Pongal) festival in January, to venerate the sun and the cattle and to renew social ties. Morning and evening processions of the deities in gorgeous attire are taken out in their ornate vehicles, which illustrate their stories in a particular sequence. The Brahmotsava culminates in the marriage of Siva and Parvati. In this ten-day long festival, the car festival is the most remarkable, as the deities are taken out in their respective chariots through the main streets of cities. Such car festivals are common to all temples. Yet, in centres like Puri in Orissa and Tiruvarur in Tamil Nadu special importance is attached to the car festival ceremonies due to their close association with royalty, such as the medieval Eastern Gangas and Gajapatis of Orissa and the Cholas of the Tamil region. Processional images in bronze thus became a major part of the temple's iconography and ritual.

■ *Navaratri:* The Navaratri or nine nights' festival, prior to Dussehra, is celebrated in all temples, particularly those of goddesses, as it is associated with the story of Durga slaying the buffalo-demon, Mahisha. In north India, it takes the form of a public celebration of Rama's victory over the ten-headed demon king Ravana (a Vishnu incarnation) and the beheading of Ravana by Rama at the end of the *Ramayana* war. On Dussehra, the tenth day, effigies of Ravana and his brothers are burnt in public places.

Above: The silver umbrella, one of the auspicious symbols and emblems of sovereignty, presented to the deity during ritual worship.

Below: Special silver plates for burning camphor are waved in front of the deity, as part of the ritual.

■ *Vasantotsava:* Associated with the marriage of Siva and Parvati, the Vasantotsava, a spring festival, is celebrated in all Saiva temples in spring. A union through marriage suggests regeneration in every sphere of human endeavour. The worship of Kama, the God of Love, who embodies potency and fertility, and the annual renewal of spring, is the main focus of the festival. This festival has no sectarian origin or emphasis. Coming at the end of winter, it celebrates many things, particularly the warmth and light of spring, and hence, is common to Saiva, Vaishnava and other cults. Kama has no definitive mythology, but is associated with Siva's marriage, which takes place after Parvati's penance. Kama tries to play Cupid and unite Siva and Parvati for procreation, incurs the wrath of Siva, who is disturbed in his meditation and curses Kama (who dies), and then revives him at the request of Parvati, whom Siva marries. Hence, it is both a rejuvenation and a marriage myth. The Vasantotsava emphasises fertility, while the motif of sexual creation spans both cosmic and temporal spheres. Hence, the re-enactment of divine marriage and cosmic sexual intercourse is repeated at these festivals.

The Vaishnava tradition associates Kama with Pradyumna, Krishna's son, and links the spring festival of ancient and medieval times to the present day Holi, wherein Krishna is the central figure. It is very popular in Mathura (Brindavan in Uttar Pradesh), Krishna's birthplace, and in Rajasthan where Krishna legends and his dalliance with the cowherdesses are symbolised

in the *Rasalila* dance. The modern form of this festival perhaps dates from the 17th century, when the Gosvamins, missionaries of the Krishna devotional movement, migrated to Mathura and transformed it into a centre for Krishna devotion.

The Vasantotsava responds to a variety of human concerns. In the sphere of politics, it is a means to celebrate and reinforce the power of the king. In the Sanskrit context, the spring festival is celebrated for the sustenance of the power of the king and his Brahmana officials. In the social sphere, it marks the annual renewal of society through the breakdown and reorganisation of social structures; in the sphere of religion, it celebrates the exploits of the gods, establishing a link between the behaviour of gods and that of mortals, with human marriages emulating divine marriages. Themes of rejuvenation and renewal resonate between the gods and human society, between nature and human society, and between kings and subjects.

Other Festivals

Teppam or the float festival is special in the south Indian temples of Vishnu and Siva. Images of the deities are taken out on a float (ornate barge) in the local tank of a temple on festive occasions, to the accompaniment of music and rituals. The festival of the god going on a hunt is enacted in many temples, particularly in Tiruvannamalai, where it is repeated twice a year during ten-day festivals at the winter and summer solstices. It is the ritual enactment of the royal hunt on the uncultivated borders of the settlement where the sovereign (in old times, the king) is god. On Karttikai day (November-December), a fire is lighted on the summit of a hill to commemorate Siva's manifestation as a column of fire, especially on the day of the Sivaratri festival.

There are several other festivals celebrated throughout the country, a significant one being Diwali or Deepavali. This is celebrated all over the country to commemorate the return of Rama to Ayodhya after slaying the ten-headed demon, Ravana. On this day, earthen lamps are lit in all Indian homes to signify the triumph of good over evil. In north India, this coincides with Lakshmi (Goddess of wealth and prosperity) puja while in Bengal, on Diwali, Kali (a ferocious aspect of Sakti or the mother goddess) puja is performed with great pomp.

Pilgrimage

Tirtha or pilgrimage means a ford, a passage and also water, the purifying element. *Tirtha yatra* is the arduous journey to holy shrines to acquire prosperity, merit, release from sin in this world, and to prepare oneself for salvation. To the devotee and pilgrim, the temple is a *tirtha* enhanced by art. A Hindu temple is meant to be seen; the purpose of visiting a temple is to look at it and perceive it as the seat, abode and body of divinity, and to worship that divinity. Hence, the temple is a work of pious liberality. Its architectural design and carvings together make the temple itself an icon and a text.

Places of pilgrimage are distributed throughout India and are called *tirtha sthanas* or *kshetras*. A divine presence is also felt in many places where the gods are said to reside and play. They are installed not only in *tirthas* but also on the banks of rivers and lakes; on the seashore; at the confluence of rivers and estuaries; on hill-tops and mountain slopes; in forests, groves and gardens; near the abodes of the blessed or hermitages; in villages, towns and cities, or in any other lovely place, according to canonical texts.

The idea of pilgrimage in India has a special ritual significance as it is derived from the concept of *bhakti*. The ascetic's goal of renunciation is redefined as equivalent to *bhakti*, and hence, pilgrimage becomes a substitute for *sannyasa* (asceticism). Pilgrims aspire to attain salvation by visiting holy shrines to prepare for release from the temporal world *(moksha). Moksha* cannot be attained before fulfilling one's duty towards one's family and society. Pilgrimage thus came to be consciously promoted by traditions that have grown up around a shrine and its locale. They are used to explain and sustain the shrine's claim to sanctity. Thus arose a large corpus of literature called the *Sthala Puranas* (ancient stories of a sacred site) or *Mahatmya* (greatness of a shrine/site). While this is true of most holy centres in India, as a whole, it is in south India that a rich tradition of mythology for every shrine was developed, drawing both from the wide resources of Hindu mythology, and more particularly, from the long and uninterrupted tradition of local Tamil myths, which are highly complex and multi-layered, many of which are reworkings of Sanskrit myths.

Pilgrims' literature grew around hundreds of shrines, each *Sthala Purana* seeking to justify pilgrimage to the particular shrine which it glorifies. The divine marriage myth of Siva and Parvati is thus central to the unification of the local goddesses as consorts of the Puranic Siva, and variants of the myth occur in several pilgrimage centres, with different mythical associations and narratives of the marriage in different areas. Thus we have Minakshi married to Sundaresvara in Madurai, and Kamakshi to Ekamranatha in Kanchi, and so on. Myths are thus associated with fertility and rebirth, sacred power, and all that power can bring – life, material prosperity and the ideal of salvation.

A sacred geography is created by the process of bringing together cult centres of a particular religious tradition through myths and symbols. In India this has happened at various levels – local, regional and pan-Indian. Cults created their own religious topography and sacred geography through links with other regional centres by means of myths and legends evolving around a specific cult. Many such cultic geographies emerged in south India between the 7th and 17th centuries

The cult of Balaji, as the famous Venkatesvara at Tirupati (a Vishnu temple) is known, acquired a pan-Indian status by being elevated to it after the Vijayanagara rulers made Venkatesvara their tutelary deity. The temple's growth as a powerful institution was due to such patronage and gifts of lands and other wealth over the centuries, and also due to the establishment there of the pontifical seat of one of the most revered spiritual leaders of the Vaishnava sect. In fact, pilgrim networks expanded in the Vijayanagara and post-Vijayanagara periods when significant reorganisation, elaboration and changes in the temple ritual and festivals, incorporating manifold Vedic and Agamic practices, took place. A legendary origin was assigned to such temples, and localisation of myths and legends, folk and other local deities was brought into their histories. Thus, fact and fabrication combined to construct the *Sthala Purana* and the *Mahatmyas*, to enhance the importance of a particular deity of an area, and to attract devotees from far and near. When royal patronage dwindled, and fluctuating local and chiefly elite patronage affected the

Jagannatha temple, Puri. The famous ratha yatra *festival of Jagannatha, the ruling deity of Kalinga (Orissa). The medieval kings of Orissa performed the* cheropahara *ritual or sweeping of the chariot at the beginning of the* ratha yatra *as servants of Jagannatha. Puri is a major pilgrim centre and attracts large crowds even today during this festival.*

fortunes of a temple, the temple's importance came to be reinforced by the pilgrimage networks of the local priestly families, and spiritual leadership, which gained access to the wealth and revenue of the temples (which had a long sacred association).

The idea of pilgrimage was also promoted as it was said to relieve tensions and resolve conflicts arising out of caste and community differences. Hence, if the Vaishnava and Saiva centres built their own pilgrimage network, there also developed a common all-India pilgrimage network, consisting of Saiva, Vaishnava, Sakta and Subrahmanya temples. Holy centres from time immemorial, located on mountains, confluences of rivers and river crossings, centres with epic associations (the *Ramayana* in particular), became a part of this network. Ayodhya, Badarinath, Kedarnath, Amarnath, Kasi (Varanasi), Puri, Dvaraka, Ramesvaram, Kanchipuram, Tirupati, Tiruvannamalai and Srirangam are some of the important places in this pilgrimage network. The list often swells with the addition of new cults which have originated in India from time to time, upto the present day, such as the cult of Santoshi Ma in north India (Gujarat and Rajasthan) and Vaishno Devi (near Katra in Jammu and Kashmir). The millenerian concept of the appearance of a spiritual leader or a great prophet, or a reincarnation of god to alleviate the suffering of humanity has always been an important part of the process of the emergence of new cults (like Sai Baba of Shirdi in Maharashtra) and new centres of worship and pilgrimage.

Temple, Sect and Community

The Puranic world view introduced several cosmologically significant concepts, crucial to the development of the Brahmanical religion and social order. One was the concept of the *yuga* or aeons, in deteriorating order due to the decline of *dharma*. The fourth and the last is the present Kali age (age of evil), when *dharma* is totally subverted. To re-establish order in the universe, the gods appeared in various forms to destroy evil and protect the world from chaos and annihilation. Closely associated with these ideas are the establishment of monarchy as the only form of political organisation to restore and protect the Brahmanical social order, based on the system of caste division (*varna jati*), with the Brahmana scholar-priest as the upholder of the ideological basis of society. Hence, the Puranic religious sects together took the position of orthodoxy against the Buddhists and Jains who opposed the Vedic-Brahmanic social order.

The Brahmanical religion served as the ideological underpinning for the evolution of a socio-political organisation and Brahmana-Kshatriya domination. Kshatriya patronage and Brahmanical legitimacy of the Kshatriya thus became mutually supportive. However, royal patronage and predilection to one or the other of the Puranic religions inevitably led to sectarian differences and conflict for patronage. Sectarianism characterised the medieval *bhakti* movements, with the temple as their focus, aimed at building their respective Puranic religious traditions and social bases. It also meant the emergence of parallel and counter structures – a community consciousness among the devotees of a particular god, cutting across social divisions based on caste, and as a means to salvation for all, irrespective of social status.

A group of Naga sanyasis performing one of their rituals. They claim that their sect was originally formed in the medieval period to fight for and protect the interests of Hindus.

Saiva spiritual lineages consolidated their organisations under royal patronage in north and central India under the many Kshatriya ruling families, and in south India under the Cholas. Among the Saivas, the Pasupata-Kalamukha-Kapalika sects represented the hedonistic forms of worship which were gradually incorporated into the mainstream Saiva tradition from the 9th century. The Saiva Siddhanta movement gained ascendancy from the 13th century, when a philosophical thrust was sought for Saivism under spiritual leaders who tried to imbibe Upanishadic ideals and influences from the north, particularly from Kashmir. This led to major canonical restructuring and the establishment of monastic traditions. Several monastic sects emerged, claiming links with major monastic orders from Varanasi and central India, and spread all over the country. Spiritual leaders of various orders tried to create community consciousness among their followers and to widen their popular base. They claimed to be custodians of the respective canons or scriptures, both in Sanskrit and in the vernacular.

Developments in the Vaishnava religion in the early medieval and medieval periods also show the same trends. Canonical texts were collected and organised, spiritual leaders and their orders created religious organisations (*mathas*) to control the temple and its administration, as also the community organisation. From the 14th century, Vaishnava religious leadership also strengthened its hold over temples and built up community organisations with wider social bases under Vijayanagara and post-Vijayanagara (Nayaka) patronage. Schisms also appeared due to emphasis on either the Sanskritic or the vernacular aspects of the canon and scriptures. Vaishnava movements took other forms in Karnataka, Maharashtra and Bengal, where emphasis was laid on *bhakti* as the only ideal, such as the Chaitanya movement of the 16th century in Bengal, focussing on Krishna, the deity par excellence of the Vaishnavas and the author of the *Bhagavad Gita*.

Philosopher-thinkers like Sankara (8th–9th century) and Ramanuja (12th century) had their own following with their widely recognised contribution in the fields of complex Hindu philosophical thought. Sankara stands at the beginning of a millennium of continuous philosophical debate and the emergence of different schools of philosophy, and Ramanuja, a social reformer and spiritual leader, was the founder of the Srivaishanava movement, introducing liberal reforms in temple organisation, ritual and administration, by including non-Brahmana elements and widening the social base of the sect.

A procession of sadhus at the Kumbh Mela at Prayag, Allahabad. The various emblems displayed by the ascetics include the silver chattar *(canopy), sceptre, trumpet and the* gaddi *(seat of honour).*

In Karnataka, social reformers like Basava and his successors, including women saints, created through the Virasaiva movement, counter structures to the Brahmanical socio-religious order of a caste-based society and attempted to establish gender equality. Yet, they also had to resort to the temple and the *matha* as the only institutional forces to widen their popular base. Their canonical traditions survive as a major social force to this day. However, while religion served initially to cut across Brahmanical caste divisions and create a sense of community in devotees, placing community above caste as a criterion of social acceptance, it also succumbed to the traditional *varna-jati* (caste system) structure. Even religious sects often crystallised into castes, such as the Vadakali and Tenkalai among the Srivaishnavas of Tamil Nadu and the Virasaivas or Lingayats of Karnataka in south India.

North India too witnessed several movements in the medieval period, emphasising *bhakti* as the means to social equality and salvation. Kabir, Tulsidas and others belong to this tradition and influenced the Sufi movement of the Islamic tradition. In Bengal, sectarian movements were spearheaded by mystics like Jayadeva (11th century) and Chaitanya (16th century) and in Maharashtra by Nimbarka and Chakradhara, also in the medieval period.

The Temple, Society, Economy and Polity

The temple in India originated as a place of worship or a cult centre, in the centuries immediately before and after the beginning of the Christian era. It was systematically built up as an institution, an innovative focus for all human activities – social, economic and cultural – and as a symbol of power by the ruling dynasties from the 4th century. The place where the deity was enshrined thus became a major concern for all aspirants to power. Hence, the art of building temples and carving images was promoted. For the upkeep of the place of worship, the temple, special provisions were made such as grants of land, cattle and gold by the rulers, to legitimise their sovereignty. Gift-giving also became the only means to acquire status in society for the land-holding elite, the merchant, the craftsmen and others in an ordered hierarchy.

In the early period of Indian history, the ritual of *yajna* (sacrifice) had a specific socio-cultural and economic context – that of a pastoral tribal society in the Vedic period (1500–600 BC), in which distribution of wealth through patronage and reciprocal acknowledgement of power was dominant. *Dana* or gift replaced *yajna* as an institutional means of exchange and distribution of wealth (land in particular) in the post-Vedic period (6th century BC onwards), and more intensively in the early historical period (3rd century BC to 3rd century AD) through institutions such as the Buddhist monastery and guild in a changing social and economic context dominated by trade and commercial activities. By the 4th century, the decline in the trading economy and the beginnings of a land-grant system brought about a major change in the socio-economic organisation, with new institutional forces and the crystallisation of a stratified agrarian society in the early medieval period (6th to 13th century AD). Puranic religion introduced the temple as the superordinate institutional means, both as a centre for worship and as an innovative focus of socio-economic and political integration during this period.

The institutionalisation of the temple dates from the Gupta period, when land grants (*brahmadeya*) to Brahmanas and religious institutions, including the Buddhist and Jain, began systematically. Land grants to Buddhist organisations are known from even before the beginning of the Christian era, but it was the recording of the grants to Brahmanas, from the Gupta period, on copper plates and stone temples, with various privileges to the donees, that marks the process of institutionalisation. The ruling elite followed the principles laid down in the *Dharma Sastra* (prescriptive code for social, political, economic and religious life) and other normative texts, as also the *Artha Sastra* (codes for economy and polity), which recommend the extension of agricultural activities and the colonisation of new areas or hitherto uncultivated areas through such grants, by settling various occupational and ethnic groups, clearing forests, extending cultivation – the managerial functions invariably assigned to the Brahmanas.

Thus a conscious attempt to integrate different kinds of human settlements into a systemic organisation through agrarian expansion was made by the ruling elite, with the ideological support of the Brahmanical priests. The temple lands thus granted were cultivated by tenants and sharecroppers and other service groups in a lord-servant relationship, often in the form of a feudal organisation. Land-owning elite like the Brahmana priests, ritual specialists and high-caste non-Brahmanas

administered temple lands on behalf of the temple, and committees were nominated to look after the various economic and ritual activities of the temple.

The temple was the major consumer of articles of everyday use and also luxury items like silk, gold and precious jewels for the deities. Royal patronage provided the resources both as an act of legitimisation of their sovereignty and territorial authority and also for the promotion of agricultural and commercial activities. Temple service thus became the only means of ensuring a place in society for many of the non-land-owning and dependent rural and urban population.

Temples were repositories of inscriptional records registering endowments of various kinds. Grants for oil and *ghee* (clarified butter) for lamps, and offerings and other rituals were made to it in the form of cattle, to ensure a continuous supply of such items. These were ostensibly meant as gifts for the merit of the donor but were of economic significance for the pastoralists who were thus integrated into temple society and economy. Such grants were redistributed among the cowherds and shepherds, who were entrusted with the responsibility of supplying the required milk products to the temples. Oil mongers as producers of oil for the temple lamps and for other purposes, weavers supplying cloth, metal workers and all occupational groups providing for the rituals and other requirements of the temple, and local merchants and itinerant traders procuring consumable items like incense, camphor, aromatic wood for rituals and luxury items like precious stones and perfumery from distant lands, were the other groups brought into the orbit of temple society. Land grants were similarly entrusted to the local assemblies of Brahmanas and the agricultural elite, who redistributed the land among tenant-cultivators to supply agricultural produce to the temple. From the 6th century, this process ushered in a systemic integration of pastoral and agricultural groups who had hitherto lived in settlements of a subsistence-level economy into a new agrarian organisation in which surplus production for the temple and land-owning elite became the basis for socio-economic relations.

This is true of practically the whole of India, but a complete picture of the pivotal role of the temple is available in the rich south Indian inscriptional records, which are numerous. In regions of commercial importance, and for long-distance trade carried on by itinerant traders, the temple again provided the institutional focus, acting not only as the recipient of gifts from traders but also often as a bank with gold and money deposits, by investing them in the production of goods of daily consumption and procurement of luxury items. These were often under the control of the local elite, the influential Brahmanas, and non-Brahmanas, who acted as executives and administrators through their assemblies called *sabhas, urs* and *nagarams*. Under powerful regional kingdoms like these of the Cholas, they were more directly supervised by royal functionaries, who audited temple accounts, checked income and expenditure, misappropriation or failure to execute grants and sometimes also re-allocated resources. Thus the effective administration of the temple was ensured through a large paraphernalia of functionaries and employees – from learned priests to menial staff. The temple, as a land-owner, employer and consumer acquired its own treasury (for gold and other deposits of a precious nature), a granary, and archives for its records.

The economic outreach of the temple, especially of those in royal and sacred centres, was impressive. Temples had educational institutions attached to them,

where Vedic and Sastric knowledge was imparted by scholars well-versed in Sanskrit and vernacular traditions, depending upon the nature of royal and elite patronage. They also received grants for the maintenance of hospitals, where the science of medicine was taught and practised. Leaders of different religious communities had their *mathas* located either within the temple precincts or in its immediate vicinity, as they came to exercise control over the temple's enormous resources in important religious centres, and fostered community consciousness among the followers of different religions, including the so-called 'heretical' Jainism, which also adopted the temple as its central institution.

Devotees sitting in the mandapa of a Siva temple after worship and paying fees (dakshina) to priests for conducting special puja to fulfil specific vows (vrata) of the families, propitiating the deity.

The temple played the most significant role in the societal change that accompanied the economic restructuring of the early medieval period. Land grants were given to the Brahmanas, who were learned scholars and teachers and comprised the highest rank among the Brahmana caste, both for their scholarly pursuits and purity. The temple priests, who were also Brahmanas, but with a lower rank in society, next to the scholarly Brahmanas, were similarly assigned lands in lieu of payment for their services in the temple (for conducting worship and other rituals), which in turn came to be shared between the priests and the cultivators entrusted with production. Dancers, musicians and other functionaries attached to the temple were given lands and houses for their services. Menial servants were paid wages again in the form of foodgrains or other consumable items, depending on the importance of their service and rank in the hierarchy. Thus, a very complex system of resource mobilisation and redistribution through the temple as the major institutional force developed and continued till the 17th–18th centuries.

The priestly order and the ruling families stood at the apex of this caste hierarchy, reinforced, in a way, by the temple organisation. Other temple service personnel and elite groups in an agrarian and an urban context were assigned ritually lower ranks, followed by crafts groups and menial service groups who were

assigned to the periphery. Such an organisation is also reflected in the morphology of a settlement or place, rural and urban, with the temple as the nucleus surrounded by a horizontal segregation of the different quarters where these social groups lived, the ritually higher in the centre, the ritually lower in the immediate surroundings, and the ritually impure (untouchables) on the outskirts of the village or city.

The priests were divided into hierarchical groups for various ceremonies and services. The main priests had to undergo a long and arduous process of *diksha* or initiation before they were admitted to the inner sanctuary to perform rituals. This was common to all priests, but was specially conspicuous in canonised temples like Chidambaram, which set a model for all Siva temples in south India. Priestly and other services tended to become hereditary as the rights of performing puja were handed down from one generation to another in the families of the priests as *kani* (rights of enjoyment). Other Brahmana ritual specialists (each known by the name associated with his/her service) had various duties assigned to them, like the lighting of lamps, bringing water for *abhisheka*, and flowers for offerings, and the preparing of food to be later distributed as *prasada* among the devotees. It was in the distribution of the *prasada* that the stratified ritual ranks of various groups was observed. The higher castes like the Brahmanas and the royal families were served first and the residue was given to the lower castes.

The non-Brahmana staff, some of whose services were required mainly at festival periods, consisted of musicians, dancers, singers, masters of ceremony, carpenters, potters, washermen, garland-makers, palanquin-bearers, administrators, guards and cleaners. This led to the multiplication of castes among temple servants, including the *devadasis* who were dancers and singers.

The temple thus stood at the centre, creating physical and active space for every aspect of life in the early and medieval periods of Indian history. Above all, it was a symbol of authority, status, political power and social influence. However, in the colonial period and post-independence era, the political, economic and social role of the temple decreased in importance due to the changing economic conditions and sources of power brought in by the advance in science and technology, and by the industrial and capitalist instruments of change. The temple retained its role as a centre of worship and pilgrimage, while its enormous lands and other properties came to be entrusted to important people (trustees) of its locality, under the strict control of government bodies such as the Hindu Religious and Charitable Endowment Board. Spiritual leaders like the Sankaracharyas – tracing their descent from the great philosopher-thinker Sankara – of different orders, however, continue to wield considerable influence over the temple's ritual and festive activities, and over the respective religious communities. This is of great importance in contemporary India, where the political abuse of religion has led to fundamentalist groups using religious symbols to perpetrate violence against other groups. This is indeed a reversal of roles for the temple, which began as an institution of social integration and cultural development and has ended up as a symbol of divisive culture in the hands of fundamentalists.

Chola temple, Gangaikondacholapuram, 11th century. A second major royal temple which symbolises power and royal splendour. The temple has a vimana *with an interesting concave outline in* dravida *style marked by its storeyed* sikhara *similar to the Tanjavur temple, but lower in height.*

Glossary

A	
abhisheka	anointing/sacred bath
achala	stationary/that which does not move
acharya	teacher
adhishthana	base
advaita	non-dualism
agamas	canonical texts on making temples and images
alankara	decoration
alasa-kanya	gentle maiden
ambalam	term used in Kerala for a temple
amlaka	myrobalan
amrita-kalaza	pot of nectar/spirituous liquor
ankurarpana	rite of germination
antarala	passage connecting the shrine to the hall
antariksha	space (mid-air)
apasmara	ignorance
apsara	celestial maiden/nymph
araiyar	male ritual dancers/specialists
archaka	priest/worshippers
archana	ritual offering
ardha mandapa	pillared hall in front of the shrine
ardra/tiruvadirai	star of god Siva
artha sastra	science of polity
astha-dikpalas	guardians of the eight directions
asvathara	frieze of horses (panel of sculpted horses)
avarana koshtha	surrounding niches on the temple walls
avatara	incarnation/descent of the god on earth
B	
bhadra-prasada	excellent structure/shrine
bhakti	devotion
bhoga	enjoyment
bhoga mandir	hall of offering/prayer
bhumi	earth/level/stage
brahmadeya	grant to brahmanas, usually land
brahman	universal soul
brahmana	the priestly caste
Brahmasthana	the centre of the *Vastumandala* for the main deity
Brahmotsava	the major annual festival in a temple, believed to be performed by Brahma
C	
chaitya	a Buddhist shrine/an architectural motif
chala	that which moves/mobile
chandrika	moonstone (capstone)
cheropahara	the rite of sweeping the temple chariot
D	
dana	gift
darsana	view/sight
dasa-tala	a scale or measurement for images
devadana	gift to a temple or deity, usually of land
devadasi/ devaradiyar	slaves or servants of god (temple dancers)
dharma	a code of conduct
dharma sastra	the norms of social/political behaviour
dhruvabhera	the fixed deity in the main shrine

dhyana-sloka	memorised verse
dikpalas	guardians of the directions
diksha	the rite of initiation
dolmen	a structure type of the megalithic burials
dravida	an architectural style
dvarpala	doorkeeper
dvara-sakha	doorway to the sanctum
G	
ganas	flock/troop
gandharva	celestial musician, demi-god (male)
gajapitha	elephant base
garbhadana	impregnation
garbha griha	womb house (the main shrine)
gavaksha	a window above the entrance (on the tower of the shrine)
ghana-dvara	opening in a solid wall
gond	a central Indian tribe
gopura	entrance gateway to a temple
griva	the portion above the cornice of a shrine
gudha mandapa	closed hall
guru	teacher/spiritual guide
H	
hamsa	goose/swan
hiranyagarbha	golden egg
J	
jagmohana	the hall in front of the shrine
jangha	the middle portion of the temple wall
jayastambha	pillar of victory
jiva	living being
K	
kadu	forest
kakshasana	seat with a sloping back
kalasa	auspicious vessel (jar)
kalyana mandapa	marriage hall
kapalika	a Saiva sect
kapili	junction
karana	a movement in dance or acrobatics
kirtti-mukha	a motif symbolising fame
kirtti-stambha	pillar of fame
kolika	junction
krishna-lila	the sports of Krishna
kshatriya	the warrior caste (ruler)
kshetra	sacred site
kumbha-panjara	a pilaster with a pot base
L	
latina	creeper-like tower
linga	aniconic form of Siva (the phallic symbol)
lokapalas	protectors of the regions
M	
madanika	a bracket figure (female)
maha mandapa	the great hall of the temple
mandala	a yantra or geometrical device/polygon
mandapa	hall or pillared pavillion
mandovara	the wall-face upto the entablature
manjari	cluster of blossoms (the tower of a shrine)

mantra	sacred utterance	shodasa-maha-upachara	sixteen kinds of great service (worship) to god
matha	monastery	shanmata	six major Puranic cults
matulunga	pomegranate	sikhara	tower
megalith	burial structure made of huge stone	silpi	sculptor
mithuna	amorous couple	Sivaratri	the night sacred to Siva
mula-prasada	the main structure	sramana	Buddhist or Jain who performs austerity
mukha mandapa	the front porch in a temple	sthala-purana	history of a sacred centre or shrine

N

nadu	cultivated/settled area/region	sthapati	founder/establisher of a temple
naga	serpent (male)	sthira	permanent
nagara	an architectural style	stupa	Buddhist monument
nagini	serpent (female)	sudra	the fourth caste
naivedya	food offering	sukhanasa	simulated opening at the tower's first tier
nakshatra	star	sura-sundari	celestial beauty/decorative figure
narathara	frieze of human figures (sculptured panel)	sutradhara	designer
nata mandir	hall of dance	sutragrahi	surveyor, one who knows the rules
natya	dance	svargarohana	memorial/ascent to heaven
natyacharya	teacher of dance (master)		

T

navaranga	hall infront of the shrine	tai-pusam	a festival in the Tamil month of Tai
navaratri	a festival of nine nights	takshaka	carpenter (also sculptor)
nirandhara prasada	shrine without an inner ambulatory	talamana	iconometry
		tenkalai	a Vaishnava sect

P

		teppam	float festival
padadevata	subsidiary deity	tirtha yatra	pilgrimage to holy sites
padmasila	lotus-stone	tiruvonam	star of Vishnu
panchayatana	five shrines for five deities	torana	free-standing gate (a decorative arch)

U

parivara-devata	deities of a family/pantheon		
parivettai	the festival of hunting	upachara	service
parsvadevata	chief images placed in the temple niches	upanishad	a philosophical system
pasupata	a Saiva sect	urah sringa	miniature shrine on the tower of the shrine
pitha	socle/pedestal/base		

V

pradakshina	circumambulation – a ritual	vahana mandapa	hall for the vehicles of the deity
prakara	courtyard/enclosure	vaikhanasa	a Vaishnava canonical tradition
prasadam	the remainder of the offering to god distributed among the devotees	vaisya	the third caste (of the brahmanical social order)
prasada	structure/term to denote a temple	vajralepa	hard mortar (diamond plaster)
pratihara	doorkeeper	vandana-malika	floral garland as decorative arch
puja	ritual worship	varddhaki	carpenter (builder-plasterer-painter)
Puranas	brahmanical religious/canonical texts	varna-jati	the caste organisation
		vastupurusha-mandal	the cosmological plan of the temple

R

rahasya	hidden/secret	Vastu Satsra	the science of architecture
rajopachara	service/attending to the king	vatakalai	a Vaishanava sect
rakshasa	demon/horned heads	vedas	the earliest known scriptures in Sanskrit
ranga mandapa	hall of ceremonies/music and dance etc.	vedanta	the earliest system of Indian philosophy
rasa-lila	amorous sports of Krishna	vedi	the square Vedic altar for sacrifice
ratha	chariot/carriage	vesara	an architectural style
rekha-sikhara	pyramidal-curvilinear tower	vidyadhara	celestial being (male)

S

		vihara	Buddhist monastery
sabha	assembly/court/meeting hall	vilva	plant sacred to Siva (aegle marmelosa)
Saiva Siddhanta	A Saiva system of philosophy	vimana	the shrine with its tower
sakta	a goddess cult	visishta-advaita	qualified non-dualism (philosophical system)
salabhanjika	bracket figure (usually a tree nymph)	vyala	a mythical animal
samvarana	tiered roof	vyuha	an emanatory form of Vishnu
sandhara-prasada	shrine with inner ambulatory (double-walled shrine)		

Y

sandhya	twilight	yajamana	patron
sannyasa	renunciation	yajna	sacrifice
sapta matrika	seven divine mothers	yantra	a device usually for rituals
sardula	a mythical (hybrid) lion and bird form	yogini	female divinity

Further Readings

Banerjea, J.N. *The Development of Hindu Iconography,* Calcutta, 2nd edition, 1956.

Brown, Percy. *Indian Architecture, Hindu and Buddhist,* Vol. 1, 2nd edition, Taraporewala, Bombay, 1942.

Champakalakshmi, R. 'Iconographic Programme and Political Imagery in Early Medieval Tamilakam,' in B.N. Goswamy, ed., *Indian Art: Forms, Concerns, and Development in Historical Perspective, (History of Science, Philosophy and Culture in Indian Civilization,* Vol.VI, Part 3 – Gen. Editor D.P. Chattopadhyaya). Munshiram Manoharlal, New Delhi, 2000.

Devangana Desai. *The Religious Imagery of Khajuraho,* Project for Indian Cultural Studies, Publication IV, Mumbai, 1996 (Franco-Indian Research P. Ltd.).

Harle, James C. *The Art and Architecture of the Indian Sub-continent,* Penguin Books, Harmondsworth, 1986.

Harle, James C. *Temple Gateways in South India. The Architecture and Iconography of the Chidambaram Gopuras,* Oxford, 1963.

Kramrisch, Stella. *The Hindu Temple,* 2 vols., Calcutta, 1946. Reprint 1976, Motilal Banarasidas, New Delhi.

Krishna Deva. *Temples of Khajuraho,* 2 vols., Archaeological Survey of India, New Delhi, 1990.

Meister, Michael. *Encyclopaedia of Indian Temple Architecture, South India, Lower Dravida Desa, 200 BC–AD 1324,* 2 vols.,

American Institute of Indian Studies, OUP, New Delhi, 1983.

Meister, Michael. *Encyclopaedia of Indian Architecture Upper Dravida Desa, Early Phase, AD 550–1075,* AIIS, OUP, 2 vols., New Delhi, 1986.

Meister, Michael. *Encyclopaedia of Indian Temple Architecture, North India, period of Early Maturity,* AIIS, 1991.

Michell, George. *Early Western Chalukyan Temples,* Londres, Art Archaeology Research papers, 2 vols., 1971.

Michell, George. *The Hindu Temple. An Introduction to its Meanings and Forms,* London, 1977.

Michell, George. (ed.), *Temple Towns of Tamil Nadu,* Marg Publications, Bombay, 1993.

Miller, Barbara Stoler. (ed.), *The Powers of Art: Patronage to Indian Culture,* OUP, 1992.

Pramod Chandra. (ed.), *Studies in Indian Temple Architecture,* AIIS, Varanasi, 1975.

Sarkar, H. *An Architectural Survey of Temples in Kerala,* Archaeological Survey of India, New Delhi, 1978.

Soundararajan, K.V. *The Art of South India, Tamil Nadu and Kerala,* Sundeep Prakashan, New Delhi, 1978.

Srinivasan, K.R. *Temples of South India,* National Book Trust, New Delhi, 1979.

Photo Credits

American Institute of Indian Studies: 38, 39, 44, 45; **Robin Beach:** 98-99; **Benoy K Behl:** 22, 80, 86 (top), 88
R. Champakalakshmi: 16-17; **Dr Ajay Dandekar:** 10; **Usha Kris:** Front cover, 1, 8, 18, 21, 26, 29, 53, 54-55, 56 (bottom and centre spread), 58, 59, 60-61, 64-65, 67, 68, 69, 70 (top), 71, 82, 83, 86 (bottom), 87 (top), 89, 90, 91, 92, 93, 94, 95, 96, 105, 107, 108-109; **V. Muthuraman:** 48-49, back cover; **Dev Nayak:** 42, 43
Porpoise Photostock: Bharat Ramamrutham: 6-7, 24-25, 72-73, 76-77; V. Muthuram: 11, 50-51, 101
Roli Books Collection: D.N. Dube: 20, 84, 87 (bottom); Ashok Khanna: 97;
Roli Books: Front cover flap, 2-3, 4, 9, 30-31, 32, 33, 34, 35, 37, 52, 70 (bottom), 74-75, 78, 81, 85, 102, 103, 104;
Ganesh Saili: 5, 46-47; **Sondeep Shankar:** 23
Dr Suresh Vasant: 12-13, 19, 36, 57 (bottom), 62, 63, 66, endpaper, back cover flap; **B.P.S. Walia:** 41
Diagrams: *Vastupurshamandala* 12, 14, 15, *The Hindu Temple* by Stella Kramrisch
Plan of Kailasanatha temple: 12, *L'Iconographie de Subrahmanya au Tamilnad* by Dr Francoise L'Hernault published by Institut Francais D'Indology, Pondicherry 1978

Acknowledgement

Usha Kris wishes to thank The Archaeological Society of India for its cooperation and permission to photograph various sites.